51 Tools for Transforming your Training

51 Tools for Transforming your Training

Bringing Brain-Friendly Learning to Life

KIMBERLEY HARE AND LARRY REYNOLDS

Gower

Published by

Gower Publishing Limited   Gower Publishing Company
Gower House   131 Main Street
Croft Road   Burlington, VT 05401-5600 USA
Aldershot
Hampshire GU11 3HR
England

Kimberley Hare and Larry Reynolds have asserted their right under the Copyright, Designs and Patents Act 1988 to be identified as the authors of this work.

British Library Cataloguing in Publication Data
Hare, Kimberley
  51 tools for transforming your training : bringing
  brain-friendly learning to life
  1.Employees – Training of
  I.Title II. Reynolds, Larry, 1956–   III. Fifty-one tools for
  transforming your training
  658.3'12404

ISBN 0 566 08410 4   Looseleaf
ISBN 0 566 08455 4   Hardback

Library of Congress Cataloging-in-Publication Data

Hare, Kimberley
  51 tools for transforming your training : bringing brain-friendly learning to life/Kimberley
  Hare and Larry Reynolds.
    p. cm.
  Includes bibliographical references.
  ISBN 0–566–08410–4
    1. Training. 2. Learning. 3. Employees--Training of. I. Title: Fifty one tools for
  transforming your training. II. Reynolds, Larry. III. Title.

LB1027.47 .H37 2001
658.3'1245--dc21
                                                                        2001040540

Typeset in 10 point Leawood Book by Wileman Design
and printed in Great Britain by Bookcraft Ltd, Midsomer Norton, Bath.

Contents

Introduction

We want you to take away from this manual a rich smorgasbord of ideas, tools and practical strategies you can apply in your own particular situation. If brain-friendly learning is new to you, we can reassure you that you are joining a growing number of facilitators, consultants and coaches who share a common interest in how to bring the best in learning to the business community. And, of course, there is still much waiting to be learned.

More than a set of techniques

Brain-friendly learning (BFL) is not about techniques and gimmicks. It is far more than just putting on baroque music or playing fun games. It's a movement rather than a method. A movement to recover the real joy of learning – combining sizzle *with* substance – and helping people become even more outstanding at the work they have chosen to do.

Brain-friendly learning requires a profound belief in the joy, the wonder and the possibilities of human learning.

If you have any questions about this manual, you can e-mail us at:

questions@kaizen-training.com

and we'll reply to you as soon as we can. We'll look for common themes and incorporate them into the frequently asked questions of the next edition of this manual.

What is this manual all about?

Training has come a long way in recent years. Gone are the days when an instructor stood at the overhead projector and droned on for hours on end. These days you're much more likely to see participants taking part in activities that involve them moving around a training room which is full of colour and life. The air is fresh and there's a buzz of activity. There is lots of laughter, and maybe music is playing in the background. People are interacting, asking questions, suggesting answers and taking notes.

Of course, just because a training course is filled with fun and activity, it doesn't necessarily guarantee more learning. It's possible to have the sizzle without the substance. In fact, one of the reasons why trainers are put off accelerated learning is because they try to incorporate the razzamatazz without taking care to ensure that the activity supports, rather than distracts from, the learning.

We believe that learning events can be enjoyable *and* full of significant and long-lasting learning. We call this approach brain-friendly learning – it is learning designed to be in harmony with the way in which our brains work.

Designing training events which are both enjoyable and full of powerful learning requires considerable skill and expertise, and there are a number of ways in which you can develop this expertise. You can use trial and error. Effective in the long run, but very slow. You can hang around with very experienced trainers and copy what works. Again, effective, but you may not have the time or the opportunity to do this. Or you can use this manual . . .

This manual is designed to enable you to learn how to design and deliver brain-friendly learning. It is designed to be used, not just read. Here's how it works.

Part One, 'Principles of Brain-friendly Learning' will help you understand the philosophy of BFL. It's a common misconception that BFL is just a series of techniques – ordinary training which is somehow spiced up with a bit of music and movement. BFL is a different way of thinking about learning. Find out more in Part One.

Part Two, 'Brain-friendly Design', gets right to the heart of the matter; if you are designing a learning event from scratch, how do you do it? We've studied the best trainers, teachers and facilitators of learning, and we've identified a common pattern in the way they design learning events. Learn how you can use this pattern in Part Two.

Part Three, 'Tools for Brain-friendly Learning', consists of 51 tools you can use to make any learning event brain-friendly. Some of them may already be familiar to you, and many will not. The idea is that, each time you lead a learning event, you can dip into this part of the manual, and find another good idea for making it even more effective and even more brain-friendly.

You'll notice some common elements running through this manual:

○ There are chunks of text and diagrams which explain the concepts of BFL. You are reading one such chunk right now!

○ There are 'brain boxes' which explain why a particular concept or tools makes sense in terms of the brain. You'll find one of these just below this text.

○ Finally, and perhaps most importantly, there are two kinds of activity. Some are designed to help you understand a particular concept in more detail. Others are designed to apply the concept to learning events that you are facilitating.

Brain box: Big picture overview

How can we understand something as complex as the human brain? Somebody once said: 'If the brain were so simple that we could understand it, we would be so simple that we couldn't!'

Your brain contains about 100 billion brain cells or neurons. Each neuron is linked to up to 10 000 other neurons. The more frequently neurons communicate with each other, the stronger the connections become – in the same way that the more frequently people walk across a patch of grass the more definite the path becomes.

Learning is the creation and strengthening of connections between neurons. The stronger the connection, the more permanent the learning. That is why repetition generally helps learning.

Another way to help learning is to give a big-picture overview, before going into all the details. It's almost as if the big picture overview gives a kind of scaffolding on which to hang the rest of the learning. In neurological terms, it's easier to create new connections if there are some good connections already in place. In most learning events, it's helpful to begin with an overview of the whole subject matter rather than plunging straight into all the details – and, of course, that's what we're doing in this introduction.

This manual is aimed squarely at people who organize learning events in a business context. You might be called a trainer, a consultant, a learning and development manager or one of many other names. You might organize training courses, distance learning, coaching sessions, computer-based training or any other kind of learning activity. For reasons which are explained in Part One of this manual, we will use the terms 'facilitator' and 'learning events'.

Activity: Troubleshooter

Use this troubleshooter to identify your priorities in using this manual.

Statement	Relevant sections of this manual	Page
1. I need to improve 'transfer of learning' back to the job	Keep it real!	19
2. I need to raise the credibility of training by finding better ways of linking learning to real businesss results	Keep it real!	19
3. Participants need more compelling personal learning goals for a particular training event	Keep it real!	19
4. I'd like tools to enable us to design learning experiences more quickly and elegantly	Designing brain-friendly learning – Part Two	47
5. I'd like more ways of raising the energy and motivation levels of my groups. Our courses need more 'sizzle'	State is everything Part Three, 'Tools for Brain-friendly learning'	179
6. Our designs need to take more account of individual learning styles and preferences	Honour uniqueness	129
7. I'd like our designs to be more participative	Facilitate creation not consumption	22
8. Our training environment needs to become more conducive to learning	Rich and multisensory	32
9. I'd like to rediscover my own passion as a trainer – things are feeling a bit 'stale'	State is everything Part Three, 'Tools for Brain-friendly learning'	179
10. I want to understand the implications of the latest research into how brains learn	Part One, 'Principles of Brain-friendly Learning'	7

Brain quiz

Note: The answers to this quiz are all contained within this manual.

1. What can increase milk production in cows, change brainwave patterns, relieve pain, entrain biorhythms, alter hormone levels, reduce stress and increase learning by engaging the limbic system?

2. How many brain cells (neurons) does the average human being have? (Give or take a few!)

   a) 100 000   b) 1 million   c) 100 million   d) 100 billion

3. How many brain cells is a 12-week old human embryo developing per second?

   a) 20   b) 200   c) 2 000

4. According to Professor Petr Kouzmich Anokhin, how many potential connections are there between neurons in the brain?

5. Acetylcholine is important for booting up the brain, transmitting signals, and long- and short-term memory. Name one common food that allows your body to make this amino acid.

6. The following have all been used as metaphors for the brain. Which one most reflects current thinking?

   – A city switchboard

   – An enchanted loom

   – A computer

   – A rainforest jungle

   – A hydraulic system

7. Match these three parts of the triune brain with their corresponding main focuses:

   Neocortex   Limbic/mid brain   Reptilian brain

   Survival   Quest for novelty   Hunt for pleasure

8. Polish-born Mihaly – the University of Chicago professor who has spent his life researching 'flow' states. Spell his last name!

9. List the ten kinds of intelligence identified by Professor Howard Gardner.

Principles of brain-friendly learning

How to use Part One of the manual

Part One of the manual will help you understand what brain-friendly learning is all about.

The first section, 'Brain-friendly learning from the outside in', contains concepts and activities which demonstrate that nineteenth-century models of education and training may not be the most appropriate for the twenty-first century.

The second section, 'Brain-friendly learning from the inside out', takes you on a journey into the most complex structure in the universe – your amazing brain.

The remaining sections enable you to explore in detail the five principles of brain-friendly learning, which are:

- ○ Keep it real!
- ○ Facilitate creation not consumption
- ○ Honour uniqueness
- ○ Make it rich and multisensory
- ○ State is everything (well . . . almost!).

Brain-friendly learning from the outside in

What is brain-friendly learning? It's a philosophy, a movement and a wide variety of learning techniques for making learning (and the design of learning) faster, more fun and more effective.

Brain-friendly learning is based on the way in which people naturally learn, and seeks to recover the joy in learning that is missing for many people.

The nineteenth and twentieth centuries gave us many great gifts, but it also gave us the following models and paradigms:

- the factory model – assembly lines and compartmentalization
- the teacher as 'expert'
- behaviourism and rat psychology (reward and punishment systems) – the 'teacher' provides the stimulus, the learner learns the appropriate responses
- paternalism and bureaucratic control
- over-reliance on cognitive, 'left-brain' learning processes
- competitive approaches to learning and assessment.

All of these have left their mark on the way in which learning is designed, delivered and evaluated.

Now that we've arrived at the twenty-first century, it's time for a new paradigm.

Brain-friendly learning seeks to restore learners to the openness, flexibility, joy, sense of community and whole-bodied intelligence they had as children.

Brain-friendly learning environments tend to be positive, colourful, option-rich, collaborative, warm, multisensory and experiential.

Activity: Disease and cures

Look at the pictures overleaf showing what we believe are the five major 'diseases' of traditional training down the left-hand side, and the corresponding 'cures' on the right.

Make some notes in the middle column about what these pictures mean to you.

THE DISEASE	MY NOTES	THE CURE

By the way, this activity also serves to demonstrate an excellent brain-friendly learning technique – that of asking learners to 'make sense of' relevant pictures and images, rather than just reading lots of text. How can you use this technique? What content might be 'understood' better by images or graphics?

Theoretical underpinnings

Brain-friendly learning has evolved from integrating a whole range of developments in our thinking and culture:

○ *The latest brain research.* This has thrown into question many of our assumptions about learning – for example, we now understand much more about the role of the emotions in learning and memory.

○ *Our post-industrial culture.* We now require less ability to store and memorize information – there is much more emphasis on the ability to think, collaborate, innovate and create value out of information.

○ *Howard Gardner's challenging work on multiple intelligences*[1] – and the desirability of engaging all of these to inspire better and more lasting learning.

○ The rise of *emotional intelligence (EI or EQ)* as a critical factor in business or personal success.

○ *Powerful advances in approaches to personal change and development* – such as neuro-linguistic programming.

○ *The 'experience economy'.*[2] Consumers now expect and deserve a rich, memorable and emotionally involving experience just as much when they are 'learning' as when they are enjoying a family holiday.

○ *The decline of behaviourism* as the dominant psychology in learning, and the rise of more humanistic and holistic approaches.

○ *Research into learning styles* – one size does not fit all. The work of David Kolb,[3] Honey and Mumford[4] and Bernice McCarthy,[5] amongst others, all point to the important differences in the way people prefer to learn.

Brain-friendly learning from the inside out – your amazing brain!

○ Your brain weighs about three pounds and is no bigger than a grapefruit, but it is more complex than any other known structure in the universe.

○ The neuron is the primary building block of the brain: neurons carry electrical charges and make chemical connections to other neurons. Axons are long fibres that extend from the cell body and transmit messages. Dendrites are the short fibres surrounding the cell body that receive messages. Synapses are the tiny gaps between axons and dendrites that use chemical bridges to communicate.

○ You have about 100 billion brain cells or neurons (give or take a few!). As it grows in the womb, a 12-week old human embryo is developing about 2000 brain cells a second!

○ Compare this with an adult bee, which can do some pretty sophisticated things, such as building a honeycomb, calculating distances and communicating with other bees, and has a total of 7000 brain cells. (That's the number of brain cells grown by a human embryo in about three seconds!)

○ The total potential number of connections between cells, if written out, has been estimated at 1 followed by 10.5 million kilometres of noughts! There are more connections in the human brain than there are atoms in the universe!

○ Learning has been defined as the establishment of new synapses, or the strengthening of existing ones.

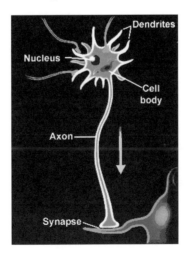

○ Learning and memory are based on the number of connections you have and how often you use them. Through repetition, nerve cells become connected and myelinated to recall information easily. Without occasional review or usage, the myeline begins to dissolve . . . *Use it or lose it!*

○ Note the following proportions of different kinds of neuron:
  – sensory neurons (perceive stimuli) <10 per cent of total
  – motor neurons (control behavioural responses) <10 per cent of total
  – interneurons (process information, detect patterns and make meaning) >80 per cent of total.

  These proportions strengthen the central principle of brain-friendly learning that training should not be about 'giving information' but rather about encouraging the making of meaning. After all, the original Latin meaning of education, 'educare', meant 'to draw forth'. Learning must be active. It must involve making meaning, not merely memorization.

○ The mind-body connection is now a proven scientific fact. At a deep level you have the ability to communicate with every single cell in your body.

The big news is that intelligence is not fixed.

Not one brain … not two brains … but three brains!

NEOCORTEX AND CEREBRUM

Comprises 80 per cent of brain. 'Thinking Cap'. Includes frontal, occipital, parietal and temporal lobes.
Wraps around the limbic brain.
Sorts messages from senses (via the limbic brain) resulting in:

◇ reasoning, reflection and cerebral thinking
◇ problem-solving and decision-making
◇ reading, translating and composing
◇ language, writing and drawing
◇ voluntary motor control.

KEY DRIVER: QUEST FOR NOVELTY

BRAIN STEM/REPTILIAN BRAIN

Comes up from spinal cord.
Monitors the physical world.
Instinctive, fast-acting and survival-oriented.

◇ dominates in fight or flight response.

Controls:

◇ sensory motor functions
◇ survival and protection
◇ reproduction
◇ territoriality and ritualistic display
◇ social and mating rituals (e.g. top dog).

KEY DRIVER: SURVIVAL/AVOIDING HARM

LIMBIC BRAIN/MID-BRAIN

Contains amygdala, hippocampus, thalamus, hypothalamus and pineal gland.
Surrounds reptilian brain.

◇ distributes messages from five senses.

Processes:

◇ emotions and feelings
◇ pleasure and attention
◇ long-term memory
◇ biorhythms – sleep, thirst and hunger
◇ sexual drive, heart rate, immune system and hormones
◇ social bonding
◇ what is 'true' and valid.

KEY DRIVER: HUNT FOR PLEASURE

The component parts of the brain

Activity: Remembering the component parts of the brain

You'll remember these component parts of the brain more easily if you:

○ read each 'card' and find out what each part does
○ think of a sound or noise that you would associate with each part
○ think of an action that encapsulates that part of the brain.

In our brain-friendly learning workshops, we have different people 'being' the different parts of the brain and then the whole group 'builds' a brain at the front of the room – each making the sound and the action.

Now make the sound and do the action as you read the information.

REPTILIAN (PRIMITIVE) BRAIN

Oldest part of brain (shared with reptiles). Monitors physical world. Instinctive and fast-acting – responsible for sensory motor functions, fight/flight, sex and mating rituals, instincts.

KEY DRIVER: SURVIVAL/AVOIDING HARM

NEOCORTEX AND CEREBRUM

Comprises 80 per cent of brain. 'Thinking Cap'. Includes frontal, occipital, parietal and temporal lobes. Wraps around the limbic brain. Sorts messages from senses (via the limbic brain) resulting in: reasoning, reflection and cerebral thinking; problem-solving and decision-making; reading, translating and composing; using language, writing and drawing; voluntary motor control.

KEY DRIVER: QUEST FOR NOVELTY

CORPUS CALLOSUM

A communications centre connecting and carrying messages between one hemisphere and another.

LEFT HEMISPHERE

Controls and receives messages from right-hand side of body. Logic, language, analysis, sequence, detail.

PROCESSES PARTS (SEQUENTIALLY)

RIGHT HEMISPHERE

Controls and receives messages from left-hand side of body. Big picture, patterns, colour, visualization, music (?), lateral creativity 'leaps', intuition, metaphor.

PROCESSES WHOLE (RANDOMLY)

RETICULAR ACTIVATING SYSTEM (RAS)

A kind of 'toggle switch' which controls which part of the brain is 'in charge'. Located in an area beginning in the upper brain stem and continuing into the lower reaches of the cerebral cortex, RAS switching occurs at one of two times: when we are emotionally charged up or when we relax. When the fight/flight response kicks in, the RAS shuts down the cerebral cortex, or learning brain. We proceed on automatic pilot, where instinct and training take over. When we are relaxed, the RAS switches the cortex back on, and allows creativity and logic to return to centre-stage.

LIMBIC (MID-) BRAIN

Sometimes called the mammalian brain, shared with mammals. Contains amygdala, hippocampus, thalamus, hypothalamus, pineal gland. Surrounds the reptilian brain. Distributes messages from five senses. Responsible for long-term memory, sexual drive, heart rate, immune system, hormones, social bonding, what is 'true' or valid, biorhythms, sleep, thirst, hunger. Primary responsible for emotions and feelings, pleasure and attention.

KEY DRIVER: HUNT FOR PLEASURE

Activity: So what?

Given what we know now about the human brain, what are the key implications for facilitators and designers of learning?

Key Implication 1

Key Implication 2

Key Implication 3

Given the above implications, what are three actions you could take to improve the way you design and deliver training in your organization?

Action 1

Action 2

Action 3

Now compare your thoughts with ours.

We believe the most important implications are as follows:

1. All learning is state-dependent. Both positive and negative emotions cause the brain to release neurotransmitters that aid memory retention. The content of the 'memory' will become neurologically associated with the 'feeling'.
2. A learning environment should be low-stress. If it is not, survival needs dominate and the neocortex temporarily shuts down.
3. We have all been underestimating the capacities of learners – we are all capable of much, much more. Raise your standards of what is possible and provide more challenge (without increasing the stress).
4. Compelling, personal learning goals ensure that the RAS keeps the neocortex switched on.
5. More than 80 per cent of the neurons in our brain are interneurons – that is, designed to detect patterns and make meaning, rather than simply take in information that has already been neatly processed. Thus, the human brain learns best when we:
   - move away from over-systematic instruction
   - use 'immersion' rather than 'presentation' methods
   - encourage questions, open-ended problems and diverse solutions
   - encourage metaphor, models and demonstrations
   - provide massive choice and variety
   - integrate different topics and disciplines
   - emphasize whole-brain methods
   - provide a rich experience – cherish complexity
   - allow (require) the learner to make the meaning.

We have blended the best of the theory and what works in practice, and created five key principles of brain-friendly learning:

- ○ Keep it real!
- ○ Facilitate creation not consumption.
- ○ Honour uniqueness.
- ○ Make it rich and multisensory.
- ○ State is everything (well . . . almost!).

Keep it real!

By the time a person leaves school at 18 years of age, he or she has experienced some 2500 days of education. How much of that is truly useful? Larry studied, amongst other things, Latin and Ancient Greek. He can honestly say that this learning has been of no practical use to him. What's perhaps even more alarming is that, at the age of 19 and the proud bearer of an 'A' level in Physics, he was unable to get the light on his bicycle to work properly!

It's easy to be sniffy about irrelevant subjects taught in schools and universities, but surely business training is more relevant? Not so. Many business training events are still organized around the teaching of models and concepts which, frankly, don't have any connection to the real business of business. According to one piece of research, less than 10 per cent of business training transfers back to the workplace.

We believe that the main reason for this is that there is often insufficient attention paid to making a strong linkage between a learning event and the real business context. How often have you led a training event where the participants show up unprepared, not having thought about the event until they walk through the training room door? How often have you asked participants to complete an action plan towards the end of the training event, knowing in your heart that only a small proportion of them will actually do any of the things on their action plan? Unless more attention is given to what happens before the learning event – what we call the '**set up**' – and what happens after – the '**set down**' – then the full value of the learning will be lost.

The first principle of brain-friendly learning is **keep it real** – make sure that there are real personal and business benefits which follow from the learning event. One of the most powerful ways of keeping it real is to pay lots of attention to the set up and set down.

Here are a few ideas for doing this – you'll find more detail in Part Three, 'Tools for Brain-friendly Learning'.

Set up

- ○ Get the participants to seek feedback on their current performance in this area so that they arrive with specific learning goals.
- ○ Get the participants to undertake a pre-task.
- ○ Get the learners to meet with their line manager and/or teams to agree learning goals.
- ○ Agree how the learning event will be evaluated.
- ○ Set up post-event work-based projects that will both apply the learning and benefit the business.

- ○ Create a carefully designed 'welcome pack'.
- ○ Use the company intranet to stimulate interest in particular learning events.

Set down

- ○ Identify specific opportunities for the participants to put the learning into action within 48 hours of the course.
- ○ Set up post-event meetings with the participants' manager to discuss learning.
- ○ Use e-mail or the intranet to reinforce learning.
- ○ Involve the learners in teaching others.
- ○ Set up action learning sets, study buddies and other support networks.
- ○ Link reward to the transfer of learning.
- ○ Place physical reminders of learning in other locations in the company.

Activity: Time to think

Imagine that you have been running a time management course for a number of years. The participants enjoy the course, but you have no evidence that it affects behaviour back at work. In fact, anecdotal evidence indicates that it has little effect.

Using some of the ideas from the list above, how could paying more attention to set up and set down improve the transfer of learning?

Here's one response. Before the course, ask the participants to complete a time log for one complete week. Give them a simple tool for analysing how they currently spend their time, so that they come with clear learning goals.

Also before the event, ask each participant to talk to four close colleagues and ask them these three questions:

- ○ In what way do you think I manage my time well?
- ○ In what way do you think I manage my time not so well?
- ○ On a scale of 0–10 how good do you consider my time management skills to be?

After the time management training:

- ○ get the participants to repeat the time log in the week following the course and notice the differences
- ○ e-mail the participants a daily time management tip for the two weeks following the course
- ○ a month after the course ask participants to go back to their four close colleagues and ask them the same questions

○ two months after the course get some of the participants to come back as guest speakers on your next run of the event.

Paying much more attention to set up and set down is the most powerful way of ensuring transfer of learning, but there are others. You can learn more in Part Three.

Brain box: Short- and long-term memory

What did you have for dinner last night? What did you have a week ago?

Most information goes into your short-term memory and is then lost. It was once fashionable to say that we store everything and that recall is the problem. There's no evidence for this. Most of what goes into our short-term memory is soon lost for ever. You can probably remember what you had for dinner yesterday because it is still in short-term memory. You are less likely to remember what you had for dinner a week ago, unless there was a particular reason for embedding that information into your long-term memory.

When we talk about short-term and long-term memory we are not talking about locations in your brain. Your brain does not have an area which holds short-term memories for a while before they are transferred to another region which is your long-term memory. Instead think of short-term memory as a fragile pattern of neurons firing, and long-term memory a more robust pattern.

The key to forming most kinds of long-term memory is rehearsal over time. There are certain kinds of memory – especially so-called episodic memories, handled by the hippocampus, and fear memories, handled by the amygdala – that don't require much rehearsal to be made permanent. But most of the learning you want to create on a training course does need rehearsal over time to make it stick. Most training courses are concerned with developing skills (termed the procedural or 'how to' memory by neuroscientists) and knowledge (semantic memory). In general terms, procedural memory requires a great deal of rehearsal to develop the skill – but, once it's developed, it's pretty permanent. Semantic memory is easily created in the short term, but requires a lot of rehearsal to make it permanent.

We use the term 'rehearsal', rather than 'repetition', to make the point that we are talking about repeating something with subtle variations and from different perspectives, rather than mindless repetition of exactly the same thing. Pure repetition is likely to lead to boredom, a drop in adrenaline levels, a decline into an unresourceful state and – well, you know what that does for learning. Rehearsal, by contrast, is doing the same thing over and again, but with variation.

Unfortunately for those of us that conduct one-day training events, an intensive burst of rehearsal over a day isn't sufficient to embed learning. It must be rehearsal over time. The precise timescale for rehearsal depends on the subject matter, but in almost every case we're talking about rehearsal over days and weeks rather than hours.

Facilitate creation not consumption

How do children learn to walk? By doing it, falling over, getting up and trying again until they are successful. How can adults help children to walk? Giving them lectures on locomotion, muscle tone and balance probably doesn't help much. What does help is providing a good environment for walking (a safe place for mistakes, a few things to hold on to) and plenty of encouragement. The fact is, when it comes to teaching a child how to walk, you can't do the learning for her – she has to do it for herself.

The same is true of adults. You can't do the learning for them. Learning is a process that happens inside their brain, not inside yours. All you can do is to create a good environment for learning (a safe place for mistakes, a few things to hold on to) and plenty of encouragement.

That's why we like the term 'facilitator', rather than 'trainer', 'teacher' or 'instructor'. Now, don't get us wrong – we're not saying that all learning has to be purely by trial and error. There is a place for giving input and sharing expertise – but input and expertise have to be kept in their place. You can't do someone else's learning for them. We like the phrase: 'keep the ball in the learner's court' coined by Dave Meier, a leading pioneer of accelerated learning in the USA (you can find his website address in the 'Further Resources' section at the end of this manual). As a rough rule of thumb, we suggest that at least 70 per cent of the time on any learning event should be taken up by the learners doing something other than focusing on the facilitator.

A training course is not something you do *to* people – or even *for* people, but *with* people. Use the 30/70 rule – learners should be doing something other than focusing on the facilitator at least 70 per cent of the time.

Make the learning *experience-based*, not materials-based. This can offer a challenge to the traditional 'instructional design' process which, in our view, often:

- ○ takes far too long (we know some organizations which take six months to design a two-day course, by which time the business need has almost certainly changed)
- ○ focuses more on the content than the process – producing heavy (and sometimes dull) tomes of written material that often intimidate learners, but make useful door props!

The menu is not the meal; the course manual is not the experience.

Don't *spoonfeed*. Pose problems rather than giving answers. Don't do for the learners what they can do for themselves, or each other – except where this frees them up to do something more important. This not only encourages more meaning-making and engagement in the learning process but also teaches people how to think for themselves, which ought to be a primary objective of business training.

Things that are created by the learners themselves are usually ten times more memorable and meaningful to them than anything created by the facilitator – whether they be presentations, handouts, job aids, checklists, quizzes and tests, stories and metaphors, role-play scenarios or process flowcharts.

Be a guide on the side, rather than a sage on the stage.

Activity: 70/30

Here's a one-day training course designed to introduce new supervisors to the company's performance appraisal scheme. The proportion of trainer time and participant activity is noted under each session. How could you revamp this course to conform to the 70/30 rule?

Session	Activity	Tutor Time	Participant Time
One	Tutor hands out company appraisal documentation and goes through it line by line. One or two participants ask occasional questions.	90%	10%
Two	Tutor tells participants how important it is to set goals. Participants then talk about their own work goals.	50%	50%
Three	Tutor tells participants how important it is to review work in a fair way. He talks through a handout on giving constructive feedback, and then participants do a short practical activity.	50%	50%
Four	Tutor tells participants that staff development and training is an integral part of the company's appraisal scheme. He hands out the company's staff development policy and asks participants for any questions.	80%	20%

ANSWER TO ACTIVITY

There are many different possible solutions – here's just one.

Session	Activity	Tutor Time	Participant Time
One	Tutor asks participants to work in groups to identify what they understand by appraisal, what they see as positive features and what possible drawbacks there might be. In the light of the discussion which follows, participants design their own performance appraisal system. Then, in groups, they compare it to the company system.	30%	70%
Two	Short tutor input on goals. Tutor demonstrates a goal-setting session with a volunteer. Participants work in pairs to do goal-setting.	20%	80%
Three	Tutor asks participants how important it is to review work in a fair way. Participants devise the principles of constructive feedback, then incorporate them into a practical activity.	30%	70%
Four	Participants work in groups to devise mini-case studies on staff development. They then come up with solutions to each others' case studies, making reference where appropriate to the company's staff development policy.	10%	90%

Honour uniqueness

Activity: How do you process information?

How many days are left until 1 January next year?

Once you have an answer, think about how you approached the problem. Did you:

- ○ open your diary?
- ○ close your eyes and picture a calendar in your head?
- ○ talk to somebody else or think about talking to someone?
- ○ sketch pictures, charts or formulae on a piece of paper?
- ○ use a calculator?
- ○ recite the mnemonic 'Thirty days hath September . . .'?
- ○ figure it all out in your head?
- ○ work it out in writing?
- ○ use another method entirely?

There are many ways of finding the answer to this problem. The way you chose to tackle it reflects the way you like to process information.

Do all people process information in the same way? Of course not. As human beings we are nothing if not idiosyncratic!

What are the implications for facilitators of learning? Given that different people learn in different ways, you will need to structure learning events to suit people's different learning styles. You could, for example, find out the different ways in which the learners on an event learned best, and then tailor a different learning activity for each learner. This might be effective, but would have two major drawbacks: first, it would be very time-consuming, and, second, no one would have an opportunity to learn new ways to learn – a valuable experience in itself.

There is a better way. In any learning event, structure all the learning to suit the whole range of ways in which people learn. In this way, everyone is able to learn in their preferred way, and they are also exposed to unfamiliar methods at the same time. As you will learn as you work through this manual, repeating the same learning in different modes is extremely effective. It's like offering a buffet instead of a single meal. People can choose their favourite food but also the opportunity to nibble at things that are a little less familiar to them.

There are many different methods of identifying the different ways in which people learn. In Part Three you will find a variety of models. One of the most useful is the concept of multiple intelligences.

How many different ways can you measure intelligence? Traditional IQ ('Intelligence Quotient') tests are obviously one method. The trouble is, a high IQ doesn't seem to be a very good predictor of business success. If it were, companies would forget about job interviews, assessment centres and the like, and appoint new staff solely on the basis of having a high IQ score. There's obviously more to being smart than just IQ.

In 1996 Daniel Goleman, in a highly influential book *Emotional Intelligence*,[6] proposed the idea that being able to relate to other people and understand one's own emotions were also forms of intelligence. Not only have his ideas made a big impact on the world of business, but they also neatly complement the work of Harvard psychologist Howard Gardner[1] who proposes that there are at least *ten* distinct forms of intelligence – distinct in the sense that they are responsible for different forms of human endeavour, and take place in different parts of the brain.

The new model of intelligence

TRADITIONAL INTELLIGENCE	BRAIN-FRIENDLY INTELLIGENCE
Standard and fixed for life	Multifaceted
IQ as barometer	Multiple intelligences, all of which can be built
Labels – 'slow' or 'smart'	Avoids labelling
Heavy bias towards mathematical/analytical and verbal/linguistic intelligences	All intelligences equally valued and nurtured
Grades and ability = bell-shaped curve	Only valid comparison is with self
Zero sum – win–lose game	Win–win – all can succeed

According to Howard Gardner's earlier research, there are eight distinct intelligences. (He later amended this to ten, but research still continues.) As you read more about each of the eight, draw a picture or icon in the box to the right of the description – it will help you to fix each definition in your mind.

VERBAL/LINGUISTIC

Whenever you read, write or talk you are using your linguistic intelligence. That is, the ability to summarize a thought in a few well-chosen words. Shakespeare was obviously no slouch in this department, and neither was Churchill. Linguistic intelligence is of great importance, measured in part by traditional IQ tests, and somewhat overused in most training and learning events.

LOGICAL/MATHEMATICAL

Can you spot the logical flaw in an argument? Are you at ease with numbers? Then you are gifted with logical/mathematical intelligence, the other kind of smartness measured by IQ tests. The patent clerk from Geneva, Albert Einstein, is an obvious example. As Ian Dury once sang, 'Einstein can't be classed as witless, he said atoms were the littlest'.

INTERPERSONAL

You may read books on quantum mechanics for pleasure, but this doesn't necessarily mean that you get on terribly well with other people. This requires interpersonal intelligence – the ability to build rapport, motivate, influence and generally hit it off with other human beings. Great leaders have this intelligence in abundance.

INTRAPERSONAL

Relating well to other people isn't the same as understanding your own emotional inner life. Monkeys are arguably reasonably well endowed with some kind of interpersonal skills, but they'd be hard pushed to do much in the way of self-reflection. Intrapersonal intelligence is the ability to be self-aware.

MUSICAL

Whether or not we can sing in perfect pitch, we all have the ability to distinguish between the tune of 'Happy Birthday' and a Beethoven symphony; as such, we all have musical intelligence, if not to the degree of a Mozart or a Miles Davis.

VISUAL/SPATIAL

We all have visual/spatial intelligence to the extent that we can distinguish between a square and a circle. Artists just have it to a greater degree. Isn't it uncanny, eerie even, that van Gogh produced such work with no formal artistic training?

BODILY/KINAESTHETIC

Anyone who is good with their hands, or body, has this intelligence – dancers, carpenters, surgeons and footballers to mention but a few. It is the intelligence of physical movement.

NATURALIST

When our distant ancestors were struggling to survive on the African savannah this was the key intelligence – an ability to understand the natural environment. A hundred thousand years later the ecological movement has underlined the importance of this skill.

To summarize: traditional IQ tests measure two kinds of intelligence – linguistic and logical/mathematical. EQ adds to the list interpersonal intelligence – the ability to relate well to others – and intrapersonal intelligence – the ability to know oneself. Then there are the artistic intelligences – musical, visual/spatial and bodily feeling. Finally, there is the naturalist intelligence – the ability to understand the bigger ecological system.

Activity: Who exemplifies which intelligence?

Which of the eight intelligences would you expect the following people to excel at?

- ○ Darcey Bussell, ballet dancer
- ○ David Bellamy, botanist
- ○ John Betjeman, poet
- ○ Nigel Kennedy, violinist
- ○ Mr Spock, from *Star Trek*
- ○ Damien Hurst, artist
- ○ Claire Rayner, agony aunt
- ○ Sigmund Freud, psychoanalyst.

ANSWER TO ACTIVITY

While it is important to recognize that all of these people have all eight intelligences to some degree (with the possible exception of Mr Spock!), we would expect them to excel as follows:

Darcey Bussell, ballet dancer – bodily feeling; David Bellamy, botanist – naturalist; John Betjeman, poet – linguistic; Nigel Kennedy, violinist – musical; Mr Spock, from *Star Trek* – logical/mathematical; Damien Hurst, artist – visual/spatial; Claire Rayner, agony aunt – interpersonal; Sigmund Freud, psychoanalyst – intrapersonal.

Activity: Which activity engages which intelligence?

Here are eight activities, which might occur as part of a training session in customer care. Assuming that each activity appeals primarily to one of the eight intelligences, which intelligence is it?

1. Ask the participants to compose a song which incorporates the key messages about good customer care.
2. Ask the participants to find a quiet spot and take a few moments on their own to reflect on how they personally respond to poor customer care.
3. Get the participants to examine two sets of company accounts, before and after a major customer care training initiative. Ask them to calculate the financial benefit to the company.
4. A role-play on how to handle customer complaints.
5. Ask the participants to give a well-structured ten-minute talk on the key principles of customer care.
6. Ask the participants to prepare a poster about customer care, using crayons and felt-tip pens.
7. Ask groups to devise and perform mimes representing good and bad customer service.
8. Send the participants for a walk around a nearby park. Ask them to return with an observation from natural history that is a metaphor for good or bad customer service.

ANSWERS TO ACTIVITY

Again, it is important to note that most of these activities appeal to more than one intelligence. However, the primary appeal is as follows:

1. musical
2. intrapersonal
3. logical/mathematical
4. interpersonal
5. linguistic
6. visual/spatial
7. bodily feeling
8. naturalist.

You could remember these eight intelligences through the acronym:

Loveable Lads In India Make Very Bad Noodles.

More recently, Howard Gardner has added two more intelligences to the list:

- ○ emotional
- ○ existential.

Try this as a memory device for the two newer intelligences:

Every Evening

Gardner believes that all the intelligences are of equal importance. Whilst we have strengths and preferences, all the intelligences can be developed. We like to think of intelligences as a bit like muscles – they are strengthened by exercise.

But why is the concept of multiple intelligences important for you as a facilitator? People's ability to learn depends on the degree to which the material presented to them appeals to their own preferred intelligence. Let's say you are running a training course on performance appraisal. Someone with a high IQ is more likely to be interested in research which links performance appraisal to organizational success than an emotional appeal that appraisal strengthens mutual understanding between employee and manager. The opposite will be true for someone with very high EQ. So understanding the different kinds of intelligence allows you to tailor your training more precisely to the learners' needs.

Better still, most people learn more effectively if the learning makes use of more than one intelligence. Why is it easier to learn the words of a song than it is to remember a piece of text? Because it appeals to both our linguistic intelligence and our musical intelligence. That's why we use rhymes like 'Thirty days hath September . . .' to recall complicated bits of data. It's easier.

Each successive study of human intelligence shows that we have all been vastly underestimating the capacity of learners. Part of the reason for this is that traditional education has focused mainly on two kinds of intelligence – linguistic and logical/mathematical. If you structure your learning events to appeal to *all* the intelligences, not only do you increase the likelihood that the learning will be relevant to each individual, but you increase the effectiveness of the learning for everyone.

When an athlete chooses to specialize in a particular area, they build muscle and coordination in that part of the body. If a person only ever exercised their left leg or their right shoulder, for example, you would expect those muscles to be well-developed, but the rest of the body would become wasted and weak. The best learners, like the best athletes, are those who are more rounded – those who have developed strength, stamina and muscle across all their capabilities. This gives them flexibility and choice.

Imagine an orchestra that contained only violins, or only percussion instruments, or only keyboards – the music might be technically excellent but the orchestra (and the audience) would be missing out on the huge potential beauty of different instruments playing in concert and harmony. Likewise, when the powers of different intelligences are activated together, it is like finding the code to open that particular individual's 'combination lock' of talent and intelligence.

Brain box: Honour uniqueness

It's obvious to us that people have different bodies – a clothes shop that offered only one size, or a health club that assumed everyone had the same level of physical fitness would be ludicrous – and yet it's often assumed that people's brains are pretty much the same. Of course they're not. Whilst most of the brain's neurons are in place at birth, few of the dendritic connections are in place. Intelligence depends on the number of connections that are established and this, in turn, depends on the kinds of experience a person has. The period up to the age of about six is particularly crucial – however, the human brain retains some plasticity throughout its life.

Monkeys brought up in a sensory-rich environment will have significantly more dendritic connections (and be more adept at a wide range of tasks) than monkeys brought up in an impoverished environment.

If you put an eye patch over the eye of a mammal for a critical developmental period, the mammal will be functionally blind in that eye because the appropriate neuronic connections have not been established in the brain. In humans, keeping one eye closed for just a few weeks in the first six years of life can produce a measurable deficit in sight.

One of the consequences of these developmental differences is that we each have a different portfolio of intelligences. We all possess each intelligence to a certain degree, but most of us will be more highly developed in some areas more than others.

There are enormous implications in this for parents, teachers and anyone responsible for the education of children – but that's a different story! So far as working with adults is concerned, the key implication is that people are different and learn in different ways. Honour each individual's unique learning style.

Make it rich and multisensory

Activity: True or false?

Please read the following paragraph through once:

A businessman had just turned off the lights in the store when a man appeared and demanded money. The owner opened a cash register. The contents of the cash register were scooped up, and the man sped away. A member of the police force was notified promptly.

Now, cover the paragraph with a sheet of paper and mark each of the following statements T for true, F for false and ? for insufficient information.

1. A man appeared after the owner had turned off his store lights. ☐
2. The robber was a man. ☐
3. The man did not demand money. ☐
4. The man who opened the cash register was the owner. ☐
5. The store owner scooped up the contents of the cash register and ran away. ☐
6. Someone opened a cash register. ☐
7. After the man who demanded the money scooped up the contents of the cash register, he ran away. ☐
8. While the cash register contained money, the story does not say how much. ☐
9. The robber demanded money of the owner. ☐
10. The story concerned a series of events in which only three persons are referred to: the owner of the store, a man who demanded money, and a member of the police force. ☐
11. The following events in the story are true: Someone demanded money, a cash register was opened, its contents were scooped up, and a man dashed out of the store. ☐

Once you have done that, compare your answers with the correct answers, which are as follows:

1. ? The businessman is not necessarily the owner.
2. ? We don't know that there was a robber at all.
3. F He did.
4. ? The owner may have been a woman.
5. ? The owner didn't necessarily do the scooping.

6. ☐T Someone did.

7. ☐? The man who demanded money didn't necessarily do the scooping.

8. ☐? The contents of the cash register may not have been money.

9. ☐? We still don't know if there was a robber.

10. ☐? Maybe there were four – the owner, the man, the member of the police and the businessman.

11. ☐? The man who sped away may not have left the store.

How did you do? If your score was pretty dismal, don't worry. It is rare for people to get more than three or four correct answers.

Why is this?

To begin with, brains do not work in the same way as do electronic computers. When you input data into a computer, you only need to do it once, and it will stay there until it is deliberately wiped out. When you input data into a human brain, it will not necessarily be recorded accurately the first time. This may seem so obvious as to be hardly worth saying, but think about it for a moment. Most business communication, and many training courses, are designed on the principle that if you want to communicate something, doing it just once is enough to make it stick. But, as the cash register story shows, once is not enough.

The 'True or false' activity illustrates another aspect of how the brain works. If you give a computer information with gaps, it just remains ignorant of the information you failed to supply. If you give a human brain information with gaps, it tends to fill in the gaps, making things up if necessary. That's why so many people go wrong on the cash register story: they tend to make a lot of assumptions about the scenario – the man was a robber, the cash register contained cash and so on – which, while plausible, are not actually true.

Brain box: Rich input

In recent years the computer has been the dominant metaphor for understanding the brain. But your brain is different from a computer in a number of significant ways.

First, a computer stores information as a series of ones and zeros. Information is either there or it isn't. Your brain stores information as a pattern of neurons firing. The stronger the pattern, the stronger the memory, the more permanent the learning. Although the idea that the brain is made up of cells was established at the end of the nineteenth century, it's only in the last 20 years or so that modern brain imaging techniques have shown conclusively what happens when we create or recall a memory.

Strong memories and effective learning are about creating strong firing patterns. One way to do this is to use repetition and rehearsal. Another way is to associate new learning with existing learning. The new firing patterns are all the stronger because they ride on the back of existing firing patterns. As facilitators, we can associate new learning with existing learning directly, by asking learners to recall what they already know, or indirectly, by using stories and metaphors which link new concepts to existing understanding.

A second significant difference between a computer and your brain is this! A computer stores information in the next available space of free memory; it doesn't matter where the information is stored. Your brain, by contrast, stores information topographically – that is, *where* in the brain the memory is stored helps identify *what* kind of memory it is. In fact the brain consists of a number of specialized modules, each responsible for different kinds of activity. For example, when you think about a red bus driving by, one part of your brain deals with the shape of the bus, another with its colour, another with the movement and so on.

For centuries philosophers and physicians have been debating the nature of the brain. The first real evidence that the brain has special modules dealing with specific functions came in the late nineteenth century when Paul Broca and Carl Wernicke[7] identified that damage to very specific parts of the brain caused specific types of language disorder. However, a healthy debate continued, and well into the early part of the twentieth century experimenters such as Karl Lashley[8] were claiming that their experiments on rats demonstrated that the brain operated holistically – that is, without any specialized modules.

The tide began to turn in favour of specialized modules in the 1950s when Wilder Penfield[9] applied weak electric currents directly to the brains of patients undergoing surgery (with their permission, it has to be said). He discovered that the body's entire surface is mapped out in the cortex and that stimulating, say, the ear area of the cortex gives the patient the sensation of the ear being tickled.

Conclusive proof had to wait until the application of Positron Emission Tomography (PET) and Magnetic Resonance Imaging (MRI), in the late 1980s. These techniques allow scientists, for the first time, to study brains in action. Simply by asking volunteers to undertake different tasks – looking at a familiar face for example – and noticing which areas of the brain 'light up' on the scan, scientists can map out which parts of the brain are involved in particular activities.

The implications of this topographic brain organization are very significant for facilitators. If you want to create a vivid and lasting memory, then make sure that memory is created in a multifaceted way. Create a memory that is based on colourful moving images, sounds, feelings, smells and tastes, and use the modalities that the brain finds particularly easy to remember – images of faces, for example.

A third key aspect of brain structure that has no parallel with a computer is the division between the left and right brain. We really do have two brains, linked by a bundle of nerve fibres called the corpus callosum (which may have more connections in women than in men). Our left brain tends to be logical, analytical and linguistic and our right brain creative, holistic and perceptual.

People whose corpus callosum is damaged often experience conflict between their two brains. They may experience 'alien hands' – for example, one hand reaches out to give a lover a gentle caress and the other delivers a punch instead. When one split-brain patient was asked 'What do you want to do when you graduate?', his left brain answered 'I want to be a draftsman', but his right brain gave a different response – 'automobile racer' – much to the surprise of the patient himself.

Effective learning appeals to both the left and right brain and, as a trainer, you can design learning activities for both.

Finally, computer memory is limited. To all intents and purposes, human capacity to learn isn't.

It's a jungle in there. . . . Actually, current thinking suggests that a more useful metaphor for the human brain is that of a rainforest jungle. Eric Jensen, in his highly recommended book, *Brain-Based Learning*,[10] draws the following comparisons:

> The jungle is active at times, quiet at times – but always teeming with life. The brain is similar – very active at times, much less so at others, but always alive and busy. The jungle has its own zones, regions and sectors; the underground, the streams, the ground cover, low plants and shrubs, the air, the taller plants, the trees. The brain has its own sectors too – areas that specialise in thinking, or breathing or memory or sexuality. And while the jungle changes over time, one constant remains true:

> **The law of the jungle is survival and no one's in charge!**

> The brain is best at learning what it needs to learn to survive – socially, economically, emotionally and physically.

> The jungle has no presenter, trainer or instructor. It is simply a rich, evolving system. It is messy, overlapping and inefficient in many ways. Our brain is similar – we have huge amounts of useless information stored, extinct programmes running and yet it still manages to help us survive. Just as no animal runs the jungle, no single region of the human brain is equipped to run our brain. Every part contributes to make the whole production happen. A plant may not communicate with a bird or a monkey, but is used by them for food, housing or survival. It's a mutual reliance club. The jungle is very different depending on the time of day, the weather and the season. The brain also has its own timetables and inner clock. The jungle is constantly evolving, growing more complex as it ages, just as the human brain does. The jungle is also responsive to change and can even weather a natural disaster. The human brain is also very resilient and grows and changes over time with stimulation.

> Both are extraordinarily impressive.
>
> All metaphors have consequences. The jungle metaphor can help us to make sense of many of the recent research findings about how learning happens, and why some traditional 'chalk and talk' training has been missing the point.

Now, let's consider a different kind of communication exercise.

Activity: The planets

Do you know the planets in the solar system? List, in the 'Test' column below, the nine planets in order from the sun:

Test	Post-test
1.	1.
2.	2.
3.	3.
4.	4.
5.	5.
6.	6.
7.	7.
8.	8.
9.	9.

Now let's apply a bit of brain-friendly learning to the situation.

> Imagine you are walking in the countryside. It's a lovely day, and the sun is shining in a clear blue sky. You can feel a gentle ruffle of the wind on your cheeks, and hear the sound of running water nearby. As you walk along

your path, you are slightly surprised to see a car parked in the middle of a field. It is a shiny new four-wheeled drive vehicle. As you look more closely, you notice, to your surprise, that sitting in the driving seat is Freddie Mercury, the former lead singer of Queen. You may even hear Freddie Mercury singing one of his songs. If this is not surprising enough, sitting in the passenger seat beside him is Venus, the goddess of love. She is not wearing any clothes. After a few moments, another singer appears.

It is Eartha Kitt. She climbs in the back of the car, takes out a Mars bar and begins to eat it. You can smell the distinctive sweet smell of chocolate as Eartha eats the Mars bar.

Suddenly, there is a thumping noise in the distance, as if a giant is approaching. And a giant it is. As he comes nearer, you see that it is giant Jupiter, the king of the gods. Thump, thump, thump! Jupiter climbs up on to the roofrack of the car, and as he does so the car visibly sinks on its springs. Now the car is fully loaded, it drives off, and you notice three letters on the registration plate – SUN, standing for Saturn, Uranus and Neptune. As the car drives off, you see and hear a dog chasing after it – not an ordinary dog, but Pluto, the cartoon dog.

You have now learnt the nine planets in order from the sun – Mercury, Venus, Earth, Mars, Jupiter, Saturn, Uranus, Neptune and Pluto. Just to convince yourself return to the activity and write down the nine planets in order in the column marked 'Post-test'.

Why is it so much easier to remember the planets in this activity than it is to remember the information in the cash register exercise? There are a number of differences in the way the information is presented, but the key one is that the planets story is rich and multisensory. Not only does it evoke vivid images for most people, but there are also:

- ○ sounds – the wind rustling the leaves, Jupiter's heavy footsteps
- ○ feelings – the wind against your cheeks, the pleasure of a walk in the countryside
- ○ tastes and smells – the Mars bar.

Another reason why this particular story works is because it includes faces and places. Different kinds of learning are stored in different parts of the brain. Some kinds of memory are more easily retained than others – and our brains are particularly good at learning places and faces.

Unconscious learning

Just before he switches off the engine in his car, Larry's friend Lech makes sure the car is not in gear and gives the accelerator a little blip. 'Why do you do that?' Larry asked him once. At first, Lech was a little stuck for an explanation – 'It's just a habit,' he said – but, after a little probing, we concluded that it was a trick for putting a little extra petrol in the carburettor so that the car started up easier next time. 'Do you need to do this with modern cars?' Larry asked him. 'Well, not really', Lech replied. 'In fact, I don't think this car even has a carburettor – but when I think about it, it was something my dad used to do and I guess I just picked it up from him.' When Lech's dad first learned to drive, it was a very useful habit; as car technology has developed over the years it's become redundant.

Did anyone teach Lech to blip his accelerator like this? No. Did Lech consciously learn how to do this? No – he just picked it up. A great deal of learning takes place beyond conscious awareness – and, for that reason, it's effortless. You are learning, but you're just not consciously aware of it. As a facilitator of learning, you can make the learning experience even more rich by making sure you are structuring unconscious, as well as conscious, learning.

Brain box: Our unconscious mind

People operate on the basis of skills, knowledge and beliefs to which they may have little or no conscious access. There are many scientific experiments which demonstrate that people have access to information of which they are not consciously aware. One of the most dramatic illustrations is the phenomenon of blindsight. A person who has damage to part of their primary visual cortex will not be able to see. If you hold an object in front of them, they will not be able to tell you what it is. But if you ask them to 'guess' at where it is, they will unerringly point to it. Moreover, when you tell them that their 'guesses' have been accurate, they will be amazed. It is possible to know, without being consciously aware. In the case of blindsight, although the relevant part of the visual cortex is out of action, MRI scans show that the image is being registered, out of conscious awareness.

As a facilitator, it's useful to know that people may well have knowledge, skills or beliefs, but not be aware that they have them. There are many ways of bringing unconscious information into conscious awareness, perhaps the simplest being to ask people just to guess.

Conversely, you can deliver learning directly to the person's unconscious, without them being consciously aware, by creating a trance-like state or by using embedded commands. People learning about brains usually find that *it's important to remember this*. Techniques such as speed-reading make use of the fact that the unconscious can take in information faster than the conscious mind.

In 1979 Benjamin Libet[11] conducted a very simple experiment. He wired up volunteers to an EEG machine, so that he could measure brain activity, and then asked them to lift a finger when they felt the urge to do so and to report when they became aware of this urge. Typically, the volunteers reported conscious awareness 0.2 seconds before the action, but the EEG registered a surge in brain activity around 0.55 seconds before. In other words, our conscious awareness lags approximately half a second behind external events and our unconscious actions.

When you touch a hot stove, you withdraw your hand before you have any conscious awareness that the stove is hot. When you are driving a car, you will brake in response to slowing traffic before you are consciously aware of having done so. Many skills which are practised at a high level of competence – playing sports, playing musical instruments, touch-typing, even speaking – are performed with little or no conscious involvement. Conscious awareness just isn't quick enough to handle the rapid responses needed. This is known as unconscious competence. PET and MRI require patients to lie still, so it's not yet possible to scan someone playing sport, for example, but scans of people learning simple word association games show that a large area of the cortex lights up when the task is new and requires conscious effort. When the task is practised and becomes automatic, different parts of the brain light up, and then only weakly.

Finally, have you ever wondered why a smile for a photograph never looks quite genuine? When we smile unconsciously, the instructions come from the basal ganglia; when we smile consciously, they come from the motor cortex. The different regions of the brain produce different results.

State is everything (well...almost!)

Imagine feeling tired, lethargic and bored. You are probably not going to learn very much in this state. Now imagine that you are extremely anxious and worried – perhaps even a little fearful. A different state to be sure, but again not one in which much learning will take place. Sadly, in classrooms and training venues throughout the world, even as you read these words, many people are tired, lethargic, bored or anxious, worried and fearful. And they will be learning very little – other than, perhaps, how much they dislike learning.

Now change the scene entirely. Think of a time when you had a learning experience that was enjoyable and powerful. What words describe the state you were in for this positive learning experience? Were you alert, engaged and absorbed? Were you feeling joyful, curious and excited? Did you get into this state because the learning experience was so good, or was the learning experience so good because you were in this state? Probably both are true.

The state you are in has a profound effect on your ability to learn. Not only is this intuitively true, but there are sound physiological reasons for this as well. In a nutshell, learning depends on communication between brain cells called neurons. Communication between neurons depends on certain chemicals called neurotransmitters. When you are in an unresourceful state, these neurotransmitters are absent – learning is simply not possible. A resourceful state is an absolute prerequisite for effective learning. The most important thing a facilitator can do is enable learners to get into a resourceful learning state.

 ## Activity: Your state predicts your learning experience

1. List here three positive learning experiences.

2. List here three situations when you were meant to learn, but very little learning took place (for example, a poor teacher at school, or a particularly dull training course).

3. Now, choose words from the list below to describe your state in each of these six different situations.

4. What conclusions do you draw about the importance of state in learning?

MORE RESOURCEFUL STATES?

Amused	Excellent	Jubilant	Queenly
Amorous	Ecstatic	Kindhearted	Quenched
Aroused	Easy	Kissable	Randy
Abundant	Energetic	Kooky	Ready
Amazed	Energized	Knowledgeable	Right
Awesome	Enigmatic	Kingly	Restless
Adventurous	Empowered	Loving	Rested
All right	Excited	Lighthearted	Silly
Autonomous	Free	Limber	Sexy
Bemused	Fine	Loose	Surprised
Brilliant	Fantastic	Luminous	Tasty
Bountiful	Frivolous	Magnificent	Tempted
Blooming	Funny	Magnanimous	Together
Beguiled	Feminine	Magical	Triumphant
Clever	Funky	Masterful	Tittilated
Celebratory	Grand	Marvellous	Tentimesbetter
Careful	Great	Masculine	Trusting
Cosy	Gregarious	Nice	Understood
Comfortable	Glad	Needed	Unbelievable
Carefree	Gigantic	Natural	Unstoppable
Calm	Good	Normal	Velvety
Charged	Giddy	Nurtured	Vibrant
Cheerful	Giggly	Nurturing	VaVaVoom!
Chipper	Gobsmacked	Open	Vivacious
Confused	Glutted	Passionate	Well
Congruent	Happy	Playful	Wonderful
Creative	Horny	Peaceofmind	Wacky
Crafty	Healthy	Pleasure	Wayout
Curious	Heady	Powerful	Weird
Delicious	High	Proud	Wild
Delightful	Hopeful	Primed	Wicked
Deep	Immense	Peaceful	Xtragoodtoday
Delectable	Important	Prayerful	Young
Dreamy	Intense	Protected	Youthful
Elated	Infallible	Quiet	Zen
Elegant	Joyous	Quixotic	

LESS RESOURCEFUL STATES?

Annoyed	Dead(!)	Miserable	Raw
Angry	Degraded	Morbid	Sad
Animosity	Dejected	Misunderstood	Sick
Abandoned	Defenceless	Nasty	Sorrowful
Bad	Defensive	Obliged	Sapped
Bored	Defeated	Obnoxious	Strange
Baffled	Disgruntled	Overworked	Stupid
Blue	Desperate	Overtired	Stupefied
Barren	Disgusted	Overwhelmed	Stumped
Base	Embarrassed	Offcolour	Screwy
Blah	Guarded	Offended	Terrible
Betrayed	Glutted	Old	Tricked
Cantankerous	Impotent	Pathetic	Timid
Crusty	Knackered	Pissedoff	Unsavoury
Crabby	Lethargic	Pitiful	Undertheweather
Cranky	Limited	Powerless	Wimpy
Crappy	Lazy	Possessive	Wasted
Curmudgeonly	Malevolent	Ragged	Woundup
Down	Manic	Rickety	Xenophobic
Dark	Mad	Resentful	

How are states created?

What you think about affects your state. Think about what you will be doing tomorrow. How do you feel? Chances are you'll notice a change in your feelings. Just thinking about something can change the way you feel.

But that's not the end of the story. If you are well rested and healthy you will obviously feel differently to when you are tired and ill, whatever you think about. Your physiology also affects your state.

So, which comes first? Do we experience an emotion in our brain, and then signal to our bodies to shake with fear, glow with pride or whatever? Or is it the other way round – we know we are experiencing an emotion only when the somatosensory cortex in our brains registers that something is happening in our bodies?

If you think in terms of causality, the question makes sense – either the brain causes a feeling in the body, or a bodily change causes a sensation in the brain. But thinking in terms of causality is no longer a helpful way to think about the brain, any more than it is helpful to ask whether the sun causes the earth to orbit around it, or vice versa. Instead, it is more illuminating to think in terms of systems – the sun and orbiting planets form a solar system, a rainforest constitutes an eco-system, and the brain and body together constitute a human system. Changes in any part of the system cause changes elsewhere. The brain – in the sense of that organ between our ears – and the body are all one system.

Brain box: Body and mind

The body has three internal methods of communication: the nervous, immune and endocrine systems.

The nervous system operates primarily electrically, although there is a chemical stage when neurons communicate with each other across the synaptic gap. The chemicals that do this job are called neurotransmitters.

If one of the key tasks of the nervous system is to protect you from physical damage, the key task of the immune system is to protect you from foreign material – for example, viruses. Instead of neurons, it uses white cells which communicate by means of chemicals that are, in some cases, identical to neurotransmitters – for example, endorphin, the body's own morphine. The immune system can be said to have a memory in that white cells 'remember' previous infections and deal with them differently a second time around – that's why you usually only catch childhood diseases once. The close linkages between the nervous and immune systems has led to the new field of neuro-immunology, which attracted 500 scientists to its first international congress in 1990.

The third system is the endocrine system. Parts of the body deliver instructions to other parts by releasing chemicals, which we normally refer to as hormones. Not only are some of the key signalling sites located in the brain (the hypothalamus and the pituitary gland) but the chemicals used are, in some cases, also neurotransmitters such as endorphin. Not only does the brain affect hormone release, hormones also affect the way in which the brain operates. For example, recent research in the USA demonstrated that mother rats are three times quicker than virgin rats at extricating themselves from mazes, the most likely explanation being that the raised levels of oestradiol and progesterone affect the hippocampus, which is involved in creating and retaining memories.

What are the implications of all this for facilitators? Quite simply, that paying attention to physiology is as important as psychology. The food we eat affects our learning efficiency – for example, eating protein-rich foods can increase the levels of specific neurotransmitters (which are, after all, just proteins) which in turn increases our ability to learn. Because our brains and bodies are part of the same system, mental processes can affect physical performance, just as physical activities can affect mental processes – both by changing state and by stimulating linkages in the brain. Brain gym is a good example of this (see Part Three, page 201).

The body's natural rhythms affect learning. There appears to be a 90-minute cycle in which we repeatedly go from a stage of left-brain alertness into right-brain dreaminess. Within each cycle, alternate the style: a highly focused activity followed by a more free-flowing process; periods of high activity, interspersed with periods of passive reflection.

Finally, although the role of sleep is still not fully understood, it plays a key role in learning. There is evidence that the hippocampus uses the time when we are asleep to ensure that learning is deeply embedded.

Summary activity 1

Review the five key principles of brain-friendly learning. Write a few words which sum up for you what this principle is all about.

Summary activity 2

Here are the five principles. For each one, write down a piece of music, or a style of music, which sums up this principle for you.

○ Keep it real!

○ Facilitate the flow

○ Honour uniqueness

○ Make it rich and multisensory

○ State is everything (well ... almost!)

Summary activity 3

Create a posture or a gesture which sums up, for you, each of the five principles. Incorporate these five postures or gestures into a dance movement.

Meat

The leader of the interplanetary explorer fleet reports back to the commander in chief ...

'They're made out of meat.'

'Meat?'

'There's no doubt about it. We took several aboard our vessels from different parts of the planet and probed them all the way through. They're completely meat.'

'That's impossible. What about the radio signals? The messages to the stars?'

'They use the radio waves to talk, but the signals don't come from them. The signals come from machines.'

'So who made the machines? That's who we want to contact.'

'They made the machines. That's what I'm trying to tell you. Meat made the machines.'

'That's ridiculous. How can meat make a machine? You're asking me to believe in sentient meat.'

'I'm not asking you, I'm telling you. These creatures are the only sentient race in that sector and they're made out of meat.'

'Maybe they're like the Orfolei. You know, a carbon-based intelligence that goes through a meat stage.'

'Nope. They're born meat and they die meat. We studied them for several of their life spans, which didn't take long. Do you have any idea what's the life span of meat?'

'Spare me. Okay, maybe they're only part meat. You know, like the Weddilei. A meat head with an electron plasma brain inside.'

'Nope. We thought of that, since they do have meat heads, like the Weddilei. But I told you, we probed them all the way through.'

'No brain?'

'Oh, there's a brain all right. It's just that the brain is made out of meat! That's what I've been trying to tell you.'

'So ... what does the thinking?'

'You're not getting it, are you? You're refusing to deal with what I'm telling you. The brain does the thinking. The meat.'

'Thinking meat! You're asking me to believe in thinking meat!'

'Yes, thinking meat! Conscious meat! Loving meat. Dreaming meat. The meat is the whole deal! Are you beginning to get the picture or do I have to start all over?'

From *They're Made out of Meat*, a play by Terry Bisson.

PART TWO

Brain-friendly design

An overview of the design process

Part Two starts out with an overview of the BFL design process – in three different formats to show we're honouring your uniqueness!

There's a Mind Map®, a more linear flowchart and a conversation with an experienced BFL practitioner. You can choose how you prefer to learn, or you can review all three formats for a rich re-presentation of the material.

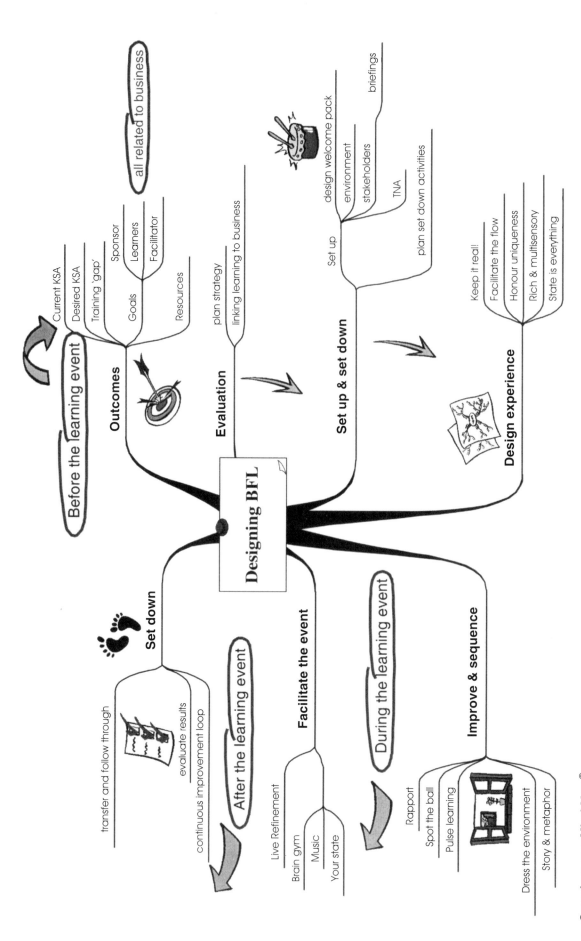

Before the learning event

Outcomes
- Current KSA
- Desired KSA
- Training 'gap'
- Goals
  - Sponsor
  - Learners
  - Facilitator
- Resources

all related to business

Evaluation
- plan strategy
- linking learning to business

Set up & set down
- Set up
  - design welcome pack
  - environment
  - stakeholders
  - TNA
  - briefings
- plan set down activities

Design experience
- Keep it real!
- Facilitate the flow
- Honour uniqueness
- Rich & multisensory
- State is everything

Designing BFL

Set down
- transfer and follow through
- evaluate results
- continuous improvement loop

After the learning event

Facilitate the event
- Live Refinement
- Brain gym
- Music
- Your state

During the learning event
- Rapport
- Spot the ball
- Pulse learning

Improve & sequence
- Dress the environment
- Story & metaphor

Overview as a Mind Map®

Overview as a flowchart

BEFORE THE LEARNING EVENT

Outcomes

- ◇ Learners
- ◇ Commissioner/sponsor
- ◇ Facilitator(s)

- ◇ Identify current capabilities (knowledge, skills, attitudes) of learner group
- ◇ Identify training gap
- ◇ Identify budgetary/resource constraints

Evaluation

- ◇ Plan evaluation strategy
- ◇ Plan set-down activities
- ◇ Link learning to business results

Design the experience

- ◇ Plan activities to achieve the planned outcomes, remembering the five principles of BFL
- ◇ Engage and inspire all the intelligences and learning style preferences

Improve and sequence

- ◇ Plan set-up and the state they walk in with
- ◇ Plan rapport-building activities
- ◇ Critical 2nd position walk-through
- ◇ Spot the ball (70/30)
- ◇ Pulse, variety and sequence
- ◇ State

Welcome

- ◇ Send out welcome packs
- ◇ Plan environment, including music and peripherals
- ◇ Design stories and metaphors

DURING THE LEARNING EVENT

Live refinement

- ◇ Rapport
- ◇ State
  - Brain gym
  - Music

AFTER THE LEARNING EVENT

Set down activities

- ◇ Transfer and follow through
- ◇ Evaluate results
- ◇ **Continuous improvement** loop

Overview as a conversation

Both of us have spent a great deal of time hanging around great facilitators of learning and studying what it is they do that makes them so good. We've also spent a lot of time talking to them, to try and work out the sort of thinking that produces such good results in the external world. Here, we give you an opportunity to eavesdrop on one of these conversations.

Q: Where do you start with designing?

A: Always with outcomes. I ask myself, 'If I could give them an injection of learning, what would they walk away with at the end of the session? What would they be able to do better? How would this help them do a better job? How would that benefit the organization?' I'm not so interested in what they will know – knowledge is not where it's at, although it might be a stepping stone along the way.

It's important that we **keep it real** – in the sense that the learning must have pay-offs both back in the business and for the people themselves. They must see the link between the learning and their own goals – whether personal, economic, social or even spiritual. Where possible, I explore with the learners and the sponsor how we can set up real work-based projects that will reinforce the learning – that's also a great way to evaluate the training.

There's a great deal you can do to set up the right learning environment before they even walk in the room, and, once I'm clear on outcomes, I'll start to design a welcome pack that speeds up the whole process. Quite often, this is designed to arouse a state of confident curiosity.

Q: And then?

A: I map out the main activities which are going to take place during the session. I'm looking for the answer to the question: 'What kind of experiences do they need to have in order to achieve the outcomes of the session?'

I aim to keep the ball in the learners' court for about 70 per cent of the whole experience – I see my role as **facilitating the flow** of experiences rather than 'teaching' or 'instructing'. I want them to make sense of the material themselves, because, then, they are far more likely to feel good about using it.

Learning is about the creation of value, not the consumption of information. Anything the learners create is ten times more powerful than things I can create, so I avoid spoonfeeding. I want an atmosphere which is high in challenge and low in stress, so I'll design with that in mind. I try to be a guide on the side, rather than a sage on the stage.

I'll pay particular attention to the first hour or so of the experience, and contracting can be very useful in setting up the right kind of learning environment.

I also place a lot of emphasis on embedding the learning, so I make sure there are learning loops – key themes and ideas are repeated in different ways at different times. And I'll nearly always design a longish integrating activity towards the end which pulls it all together.

Q: And that's it?

A: Far from it – the most important bit is still to come. I then run through the whole design, from various perspectives, and improve it. Have I got the right balance of activities? How would I feel as a participant on this course? How will I feel when I facilitate this? Those kinds of questions.

Q: How do you cope with different learning styles?

A: People are different – one size doesn't fit all. We should **honour and respect uniqueness**, not try to make everybody learn in the same way. Therefore, I need to ensure that the balance of the whole experience will engage and inspire all the different learning styles and preferences.

I use the multiple intelligences model as a simple way of checking that there's a good balance. I also find the 4-MAT model[5] a great tool. Then there's the flow . . . It seems to work best when there's a pulse – alternate switching between activities that require the conscious mind to focus, and activities with a more diffuse style that allow unconscious processing. I alternate between active and passive – right brain and left brain.

I also think about how I can make all of my input (such as a lecture) more interactive and memorable, and I try to limit my input to a maximum of 20 minutes or so at a time.

The other thing is to stay flexible and to provide choice wherever possible – everybody doesn't have to have exactly the same experience, provided they reach the desired outcome. So, where I can, I'll offer maybe two or three alternative ways of exploring a particular topic, and let the participants choose. Then, they can come back and share their learning with each other.

Q: Anything else?

A: Yes, I want the experience to be rich and memorable. One of the best ways of doing this is to create a **multisensory** experience. I dress the room – with a relevant theme if possible so that everything gets anchored to the material. Also, I try to make my language rich – to pepper what I say with a good balance of visual, auditory and kinaesthetic words and phrases.

Q: As well as creating exceptional results, you seem to have a reputation for designing learning events where people have a great time too! How do you do this?

A: Well, if the other four keys are in place, people are more likely to enjoy the experience anyway. But, for me, all learning is state-dependent. It's not just because I want people to have a great time (we spend far too much time at work not to enjoy it) but because we know it aids learning. So, I make this part of the design process.

As we move away from traditional models of instructing and teaching, I think the facilitator's role becomes more about reading and eliciting appropriate states. **State is everything (well . . . almost!)**. There's an example from a leadership course later in this Part.

Also, I ensure that I am in the most resourceful state possible when I'm facilitating. This is based on the principle that, if you are in rapport with the group, you can lead them into different states, as states are contagious. I do this by using my mental focus and my body (physiology) in ways that I know create the right results.

I have a cocktail of state 'anchors' (see Part Three) that I can fire whenever I need more of something. The lovely thing about anchors is that they get more powerful the more you use them, so these days I just 'click' into state the moment I start working with a group.

Q: And what are the states you find most useful when facilitating?

A: Well, there are many different ones, but the five I use most often are passion, curiosity, love, playful fun and a sort of calm place that I call 'zen'. I actually have these states anchored on the fingers of my right hand.

Q: And the last thing?

A: For me, the final piece is to design the stories and metaphors I'll be using during the learning experience. I like to leave this until last for two reasons: first, it's only at this point that I can best judge what kind of story will be most likely to pull the whole thing together.

Second, I like to make stories topical, where possible, so I'll scour the media for current news items – as well as examining what's going on in my own life, or the life of the organization – and look for metaphorical links between these and the material being learned.

Q: And, finally, what advice would you give to a facilitator new to brain-friendly learning?

A: First, model being a great learner yourself. Get passionate about learning. Stay curious about new developments – read widely, scour the web, and take every opportunity to participate in learning experiences. Borrow great ideas wherever you find them. Maintain a constant yet healthy dissatisfaction with what you're doing now. Seek feedback. Go for constant and never-ending improvement.

Second, I'd say becoming a successful BFL practitioner is not a mechanical skill that you can acquire without the full participation of your whole self. This is because as Dave Meier says 'BFL is not just another set of clever, creative, "fluffy" techniques that you can smear on to your old assumptions about learning – but a whole new set of assumptions.'

The important point is that BFL is systemic, not cosmetic. It's a philosophy that departs from conventional notions of learning in some significant ways. And it requires certain qualities – your whole being has to resonate with the philosophy, and you have to sense its human implications on a deep level, or everything you do with BFL will be slightly out of tune, disjointed, shallow, uninspired and (in terms of long-term value) ineffective.

Third, think about the subjects you're training. Genuine interest in your subject – even passion for it – is essential if you want to have maximum impact. If the subject doesn't turn you on, how can you expect learners to get excited about it?

It takes guts to be a leader – to exert your creativity and to break out of the grey confines of established assumptions about learning. Courage does not mean having an arrogant or prescriptive attitude about learning, but being willing to try new things, to risk failure, to 'wobble', to depart from the norm, to dare to be everything you are, and to be constantly learning yourself.

With courage you can be a positive influence in your organization – awakening yourself and others to the endless possibilities of life.

The five principles and design

The remainder of Part Two explores the five principles of BFL as applied to the learning design process. For tools, tips and detailed 'how-to's', please refer to the relevant pages in Part Three.

Principle 1: Keep it Real!

When it comes to designing learning the brain-friendly way, your first task is to ensure that there's a clear link to the business. Think about the results the business is trying to achieve rather than about 'training needs'.

Too often, training is carried out when some other intervention would be more beneficial – for example, a change in processes or systems. Even when development or learning is required, a group learning 'event' may or may not be appropriate. There are literally hundreds of ways of developing individual capability, only one of which is sending people on a course.

Once you have established a clear link between the proposed training intervention and business results, start with the end in mind – with **outcomes**.

A useful model to tighten up outcomes is the acronym POWER:

○ **P**ositive
State the outcome in the positive – what we do want, rather than what we don't want.
○ **O**wned
Outcomes should be owned by the individual learners – and should have meaning for them, for their immediate manager, for the organization, for the sponsor (and for you!).
○ **W**hat will it . . . look like, sound like, feel like?
Make the outcome sensory-specific. When the training has been successful, what will we see, hear and feel that's different from the way we are experiencing things now?
○ **E**cology
Does the outcome make sense in terms of the larger 'system' of which the learners are a part? Is this a 'wise' outcome for the organization and for the individuals? Might the outcome have any undesirable consequences that we haven't considered? Kim remembers designing a course in Creative Thinking for a public sector body which had very strict rules about the way in which things were done. The training was very successful, in the sense that participants started behaving much

more creatively in the way they marketed the organization. But the organization was horrified to discover that people also started to be much more 'creative' about 'bending' procedures, with the result that several people had to be disciplined for breaking the rules.

❍ **R***esults*

Once the learners are successfully applying the learning back on the job, what results do we want in the business? What will be the effect on sales? On customer delight or quality? On costs? On cycle time? On errors or mistakes? On staff morale or the way in which the team works together?

You can use the POWER acronym as a basis for your discussions with sponsors and learners prior to designing the learning experience.

 Quite often, views will differ about what the outcomes should be. One example that comes to mind is some financial awareness training that Kim was facilitating in a large retail organization. The line managers wanted one thing, the sponsor something else, the Finance Director another thing, and the learners something different again. This is where you can add real value by facilitating the sharing of views and creating consensus. In any case, until you've clarified outcomes, it's best not to proceed to the next stage.

CURRENT KNOWLEDGE, SKILLS AND ATTITUDES

Ask yourself the following questions:

❍ Where are the learners now?
❍ What knowledge and information do they have about the topic?
❍ What are their current level of skills?
❍ What are their attitudes and beliefs?

Once you know the learner's current knowledge, skills and attitudes (KSA) you are then in a good position to develop them.

There are many approaches that help you determine the participants' current KSA – such as diagnostics, focus groups, repertory grid and so on. Gower publishes an excellent resource pack on training needs analysis.[12]

SET UP AND SET DOWN

The set up (everything that happens prior to the learning event) and the set down (everything that happens afterwards) are extremely important, and are often neglected by trainers who focus solely on the learning event itself.

Activity: What predicts transfer of learning?

What would you guess is the most important predictor of how well learning is applied back in the workplace? Tick one of the answers below.

1. The quality of the training design ☐
2. The skills of the trainer ☐
3. The attitude of the learner's boss ☐
4. How interested the learner is in the subject ☐
5. The quality of the biscuits ☐

They're all important (with the possible exception of no. 5!), but one famous piece of research by Dr Sam Goldstein[13] showed that the most important factor is no. 3, the attitude of the learner's boss. How often have you heard managers say something like 'Back from your jolly now, are you?' or 'What you learned on the course might be all very well in theory – but that's not the way we do it in this department!'? It follows, therefore, that you should do all you can to involve line managers in your training. Consider how you can:

- ○ make sure that the training design meets outcomes that have real relevance for them
- ○ involve them in the design – perhaps by suggesting realistic activities, simulations or case studies
- ○ have them devise real work-based projects that get something important done at the same time as developing capability
- ○ involve them in the delivery – perhaps by asking them to co-facilitate or to just come along and talk to the group about their experiences
- ○ contract with them about how they will support the learner in transferring the learning back to the job
- ○ involve them in evaluation and improving the design.

Set up also includes any prebriefing of participants, sending out a welcome pack that creates positive expectations, and creating an appropriate learning environment. See Part Three for tools to deal with on these aspects.

Moving on to set down, this should be straightforward if you have clear outcomes that relate to business results. There's a whole smorgasbord of set-down activities that help with transfer of learning to be found in Part Three, Tool 2, 'Set up and set down'.

EVALUATION

The most widely used approach for evaluating training is probably the Kirkpatrick model[14] in which evaluation can be carried out at four levels:

Level 1: reactions (Did they like it?)
Level 2: learning

Level 3: transfer to the job
Level 4: organizational results.

It's probably clear by now that brain-friendly learning seeks to focus on Levels 3 and 4 wherever possible. One of the best ways of doing this is to set up real work-based projects that:

○ demonstrate the application of new learning
○ benefit the business.

You need to design your evaluation strategy up-front, so that everybody knows what success will look like. Gower publishes an excellent resource on evaluating training.[15]

Principle 2: Facilitate the flow – creation not consumption

'The mind is not a vessel to be filled ... but a fire to be ignited.'

This principle, when applied to design, is about structuring a learning experience that will lead to the achievement of your agreed outcomes. The goal is to be a guide on the side, rather than a sage on the stage. Focus on how the learners can create meaning and value for themselves. This is not to say there is no place for instruction and information-giving – there is. But you should aim for this to take up no more than about 30 per cent of the event time. The remainder of the time should be experience- and activity-based.

This principle gets right to the heart of your beliefs not only about what learning is, but also about the role of the trainer. Typically, trainers fall into one of three philosophical 'camps': humanistic, cognitive and behaviourist:

Humanistic	Cognitive	Behaviourist
Ask	Tell	Reinforce
Elicit	Transmit	Strengthen
Intrinsic motivation	Learner is 'empty vessel'	Extrinsic motivation
Learner is resourceful		Learner must be 'controlled'
'Educare' – to draw out		

Where do you sit most comfortably? Brain-friendly learning sits firmly in column 1, the humanistic camp. In Part Three, Tool 20, 'Brain-friendly beliefs about learning', there's a questionnaire you can do that will give you an insight into your current beliefs, and challenge you to explore them further.

There are also several tools in Part Three that will give you ideas on how to build a brain-friendly, total experience for learners.

MIND MAPPING® THE STRUCTURE

A Mind Map®, a term coined by Tony Buzan,[16] is a wonderful brain-friendly tool for many things – brainstorming ideas, taking notes, structuring a presentation or report, thinking and, of course, design! If you are new to Mind Maps®, see Tool 8, 'Mindblowing Mind Maps®' in Part Three.

Mind Maps® allow you, the training designer, to see the overall structure at a glance and to determine how well the design is balanced in terms of its sequencing and flow. They are also a splendid way of checking your progress when facilitating the event itself. Forget the four-ring binder with detailed trainer notes and session plans – a single Mind Map® can be your guide throughout. If you put your Mind Map® on a flipchart or large poster and stick it on the wall as a peripheral aid, it can perform the dual functions of a guide as to facilitation and a big-picture overview for the learners.

During the course, Mind Maps® are an excellent way of helping learners make patterns and work out what things mean to them.

Before beginning a new topic, ask the learners to create a Mind Map® of what they already know, and then get them to use the learning to refine and improve the Mind Map®. This gives the brain 'addresses' at which to store key information and make relationships. At the end of the course, ask learners to make large maps of their learning.

CHECK YOUR PULSE

Well-designed learning events have a rhythm, or pulse. There's a flow to them: periods of energetic activity followed by periods of quiet concentration; activities that engage the left brain, followed by activities that engage the right brain; experiences that are emotional or social in nature, interspersed with experiences that are more cognitive and intellectual. Again, turn to Part Three for more ideas.

One good way of 'checking your pulse' is to walk through the whole design from the participant's perspective and notice how it feels.

STAGES OF GROUP DEVELOPMENT

As Tuckman[17] and others have noted, groups mature over time – they are not the same group at the beginning as at the end of a learning event. Your style as a facilitator should reflect this process, and it's worth designing this in. Provide more structure and direction at the beginning of an event, and increasingly less as the group becomes more independent from you. At the beginning you will control the state of play; by the end you may be almost superfluous.

One way of providing structure that supports learning is to build in positive rituals. Paradoxically, it seems that the more 'safe' rituals people engage in, the more they feel able to stretch beyond their current boundaries (or comfort zones). Positive rituals could include:

❍ morning check-ins and special greetings
❍ cheers and applause
❍ a musical fanfare that becomes 'anchored' to the whole experience
❍ doing brain gym together
❍ songs and affirmations
❍ handshakes or hugs
❍ end-of-day rituals
❍ standing up and discussing applications with a 'buddy' at the end of each session.

THE TOPIC ITSELF

Often, the nature of the material will suggest an appropriate structure to your learning design. For example, if you're designing a workshop on statistics, it probably makes sense to have learners understand the 'mean' before you move on to what a standard deviation is.

You need to avoid spoonfeeding, however. Remember, the brain is a parallel processor (see p. 63), and we have all been vastly underestimating the capacity of learners. Also, we want a learning environment that is high in challenge (although low in stress) – giving people only bite-sized chunks one at a time can actually reduce understanding. A certain amount of confusion and complexity aids learning, and some of your learners will certainly prefer to understand the big picture first.

Activity: Design walkthrough

Once your basic design is complete, 'walk through' your course design from the perspective of a learner. It can be helpful to do this with a colleague or buddy – the important thing is that you step into their shoes, rather than staying in the 'facilitator' mindset.

For example:

❍ 'OK, so I walk into the room at 09.00 hours and the first thing I see is . . .'
❍ 'I'm unlikely to know many people, so I'm feeling a bit . . .'
❍ 'It's now 10.30 am on the first morning, and I've been sitting down for half an hour watching a PowerPoint presentation, so I feel the need to get up and do something now . . .'
❍ 'We've been working actively in small groups for two hours now . . . I'd quite like some time on my own just to reflect . . .'

And so on.

It is even more effective if you do this walk-through several times, from the different perspectives of each learning style. Now, how can you improve your design?

Principle 3: Honour uniqueness

Each brain is as unique as a fingerprint.

People are different. This may be obvious, but is so often overlooked when learning events are designed. Many traditional courses are still built around the nineteenth-century 'factory model', which assumes that everybody is the same.

People differ in many respects, and Part Three provides tools that will help you take account of some of these when designing learning events. Many readers will be familiar with the work of David Kolb[3] and Honey and Mumford[4] on learning style preferences. Brain-friendly learning takes this even further and focuses specifically on:

- right- and left-brain processing
- 4-MAT learning style preferences[6] which builds on the work of Kolb and Honey and Mumford
- multiple intelligences, discovered by Howard Gardner[1] at Harvard University
- meta-programmes.

Activity: Design walk-through

'Walk through' your course design several times, from different perspectives:

- What sort of balance is there between right- and left-brain processing?
- Is there enough in the design for each of the 4-MAT types? Are there opportunities to answer the questions 'Why?', 'What?', 'How?' and 'What if . . ?'?
- Does the design engage and inspire all the multiple intelligences?
- Have you taken account of meta-programme differences in your group?
- Now, how can you improve your design?

THIS GROUP

The ideal strategy for honouring uniqueness would be to design your learning event specifically for the individual or group who will be experiencing it.

Find out as much as you can about your group in terms of, for example:

- cultural factors
- expectations
- their likely attitudes to learning and to the topic itself
- their learning preferences.

In addition to giving you valuable information, this allows you to build rapport before the course even starts.

Strategies include:

○ sending out diagnostics (for example, learning styles preferences questionnaires)
○ telephone or face-to-face interviews with learners
○ observation *in situ*
○ talking to other people who know them.

In practice, this may not always be possible – particularly if your learning design is going to be 'rolled-out' to a large population. The practical compromise is to learn about the likely patterns of difference, and then design your event to provide maximum variety and choice.

Principle 4: Rich and multisensory

VARIETY OF LEARNING METHODS

The brain is a parallel processor – it operates on many levels at once, processing simultaneously a world of movement, emotion, colour, shape, sounds, intensity, tastes, smells and more. It assembles patterns, composes meanings and 'sorts' experiences from a very wide range of clues. It is designed to process many inputs at once (a slower, more linear pace can actually reduce understanding). It prefers rich, multimodal activities such as field trips, simulations, discussions and real-life projects.

When travelling abroad, we learn about a city from the scattered, sometimes random, sensory experience of it, rather than from a sequenced guide book. The latest research suggests that any group instruction that has been tightly and logically planned will have been wrongly constructed for most of the group, so create a richer environment – one full of variety of choice.

TUNING IN TO VHF

Some people are highly visual in the way they prefer to think and learn. Others are auditory. Still others are kinaesthetic. Part Three will not only help you design activities that appeal to each thinking preference, but also pepper your language with visual, auditory and kinaesthetic words and phrases.

DRESSING THE ENVIRONMENT

One way of creating a rich, multi-sensory learning experience is to create a rich, multisensory environment. The implicit message to the learners is that 'you matter'. The tools section suggests many ways of doing this.

MUSIC

Music has been called the universal language – and with good reason. Although research on this is still in its infancy, we believe music to be such an important learning aid that it deserves a tool all to itself. Music straddles at least two of the BFL principles – as well as being a highly effective way of enriching the environment, it also profoundly affects state.

UNCONSCIOUS LEARNING

Some researchers – for example, Dr Emile Donchin at the Champaign-Urbana campus of the University of Illinois, and Pfurtscheller and Berghold[18] say that most learning is non-conscious. Your brain is constantly learning, whether you are aware of it or not. Most of what is learned in any training course is probably not in the lesson plan.

Eric Jensen gives two examples in his book, *The Learning Brain*:[19]

1. You drive from one city to another. You arrive safely and check in to a hotel where you meet a colleague who asks you a question about something you can't quite recall. He then mentions the company's name, and suddenly a light goes on. You remember seeing a billboard on the road advertising the company, and you can now answer his question about the kinds of products this company markets. You actually learned that information hours ago – but at the time were completely unconscious of learning it.
2. Your learners are working on a project in teams. In your view (and theirs) they are learning the content. But they are also learning about each other, about themselves, about collaborating in teams. In fact, that may be the majority of the learning.

One of the reasons for using posters and peripherals is that learners will take in the 'content' of these – often subliminally.

The learning climate and environment is very important. So are your non-verbal messages. These are all 'learned' by your participants, even though you may not be 'teaching' any of them. How you treat your learners, what you say, how you say it and the room set-up are all influencing the learner and being processed non-consciously.

During the learning event, create a learning environment rich with positive suggestions. Practise using more congruent body language – for example, it's challenging to convey passion and energy congruently if you are sitting in a slumped position, breathing shallowly and gazing down at the carpet!

At the design stage, there are several things you can build in to utilize the unconscious mind, such as overloading to distract the conscious mind, creating offline 'space', using embedded commands and using stories or metaphor. You will find several tools to achieve these effects in Part Three.

Principle 5: State is everything (well . . . almost!)

The most important idea in applying this principle to learning design is that the state of the learners should be *part of your design*. Traditional instructional design almost completely overlooks this.

If the state of the learner is so vital to learning – and it is – then it follows that designers need to think about it in advance. As we have seen, state is not just about 'enjoying' the experience. It's about engaging the limbic system – and thereby enhancing recall – and it's also about making the learning state as similar as possible to the state people will be in when they are applying the learning back on the job.

The state people are in when they are learning tends to become neurologically associated with the content of the learning. The brain links the two things together.

If you're facilitating an event to develop, say, visionary leadership capability, you want people to feel inspired and inspiring both when they're learning, **and also when they return to work** and need to deliver a speech about the vision to their team.

Example Session Plan on a Leadership Course

Session	Learning Outcomes	Learning Methods	Group State (how I want them to feel during this session)
Inspiring a shared vision	At the end of the session, participants will be able to:		
	◇ list the seven common characteristics of inspiring visions – and identify these from a range of historical and contemporary figures	◇ Watch film clips of famous leaders	Inspired
	◇ write a vision statement for their own team which reflects their leadership style, will engage their constituents and meet the criteria for inspiring visions	◇ Individual reflection on the needs of their constituents	Reflective
	◇ present this to camera as a speech and receive feedback on three ways in which they could enhance it even further	◇ Group discussion on common characteristics ◇ Buddy coaching ◇ Practice plus feedback, using video	Engaged Compassionately critical Inspired, passionate and confident
	◇ make a commitment to share this vision with their teams	◇ Mental rehearsal using timeline	Committed to going back and implementing action plan

Activity: Identifying the best state for a session

Choose a session from a learning event with which you are familiar and identify the most appropriate state for the participants – the state that will maximize their learning and engagement and make it more likely that they will transfer the learning successfully.

Session	Learning Outcomes	Learning Methods	Group State (how I want them to feel during this session)

YOUR STATE

As with any other endeavour, the most important predictor of how successful you will be at designing a great learning event will be **your** state at the time. It's worth anchoring really resourceful states to the design process, so that you are at your most creative, focused, inspired or in whatever state is important to you.

Part Three provides many tools for managing your own state – both during design and delivery – as well as influencing the state of your learners.

Tools for brain-friendly learning

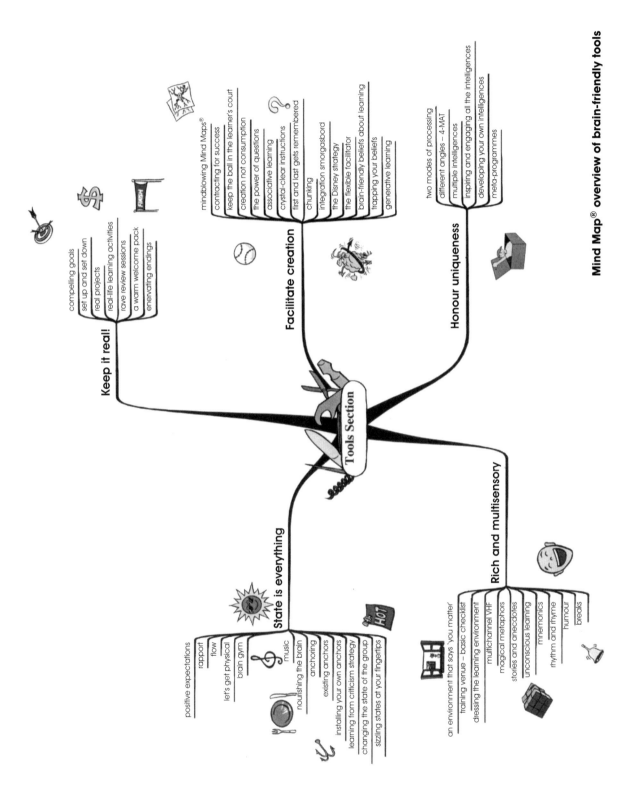

Keep it real!
- compelling goals
- set up and set down
- real projects
- real-life learning activities
- rave review sessions
- a warm welcome pack
- enervating endings

Facilitate creation
- mindblowing Mind Maps®
- contracting for success
- keep the ball in the learner's court
- creation not consumption
- the power of questions
- associative learning
- crystal-clear instructions
- first and last gets remembered
- chunking
- integration smorgasbord
- the Disney strategy
- the flexible facilitator
- brain-friendly beliefs about learning
- trapping your beliefs
- generative learning

Honour uniqueness
- two modes of processing
- different angles – 4-MAT
- multiple intelligences
- inspiring and engaging all the intelligences
- developing your own intelligences
- meta-programmes

Tools Section

State is everything
- positive expectations
- rapport
- flow
- let's get physical
- brain gym
- music
- nourishing the brain
- anchoring
- existing anchors
- installing your own anchors
- learning from criticism strategy
- changing the state of the group
- sizzling states at your fingertips

Rich and multisensory
- an environment that says 'you matter'
- training venue – basic checklist
- dressing the learning environment
- multichannel VHF
- magical metaphors
- stories and anecdotes
- unconscious learning
- mnemonics
- rhythm and rhyme
- humour
- breaks

Mind Map® overview of brain-friendly tools

Tools for keeping it real

1 Compelling goals

Why goals matter

Larry's first proper job was as a school maths teacher, and that's where he learnt the importance of goals in learning. Three times a week he took a class of 13-year olds who were struggling with every aspect of maths. One day the group were doing tables. Some of them could manage their two times table, but that was about it. Except for Paul Dobey. Paul had problems adding six and six, but he astounded everyone with his expertise at the 15 times table.

Larry: 3 × 15?

Paul: 45 sir!

Larry: 8 × 15?

Paul: 120

Larry: I don't like to be nosy, Paul, but how come you're so good at such a difficult table?

Paul: Well sir, it's easy – my Dad's a milkman and on Saturdays I help him collect the money. Ordinary milk is 15p a pint, so you just have to know how much to charge.

A child who was labelled 'remedial' at maths could be expert at mental arithmetic if he had a clear reason for doing so – a clear goal. What's true for Paul Dobey is true for the rest of us – we learn faster and more easily if we have a clear reason for doing so – a clear goal. Moreover, the goal must be one which we can relate to. A goal which provides a clear benefit to us. A goal which answers the question, 'What's in it for me?'.

Let's assume that you are running a short training session on completing expense claims. This is not the kind of session that automatically has people queuing up to attend. So what's the goal of the course? From your perspective, it is to reduce administrative errors in the processing of expense claims, but this outcome is unlikely to engage participants. You need to consider the goal of the course from the participants' perspective – in other words, you need to answer the WIIFM question. How about 'How to fill in your expense forms in half the time so that you receive the money twice as quickly!'? This is much more likely to engage the participants' interest.

Or, instead of calling a course 'Health & Safety in the Factory', call it 'Prolonging your Life!'.

Once you have identified the course goal from the participants' perspective, you can use it in a number of ways:

○ in the course title
○ in course publicity and pre-course information
○ in your introduction to the course.

As we have seen, your idea of the goal of the course may be different from that of your participants. But there may also be a third perspective – that of the person commissioning (and, in some cases, paying for) the course. What do they see as the goal?

One final note of caution – you must be confident that the course can deliver the goal promised. Beware of hyping up the benefits of the course to such an extent that they cannot realistically be realized. And, if you can't reasonably expect the course to deliver some measurable benefits, why are you running it anyway?

Activity: Compelling goals

Identify a course you are currently involved in.

1. What is the goal of this course, from your perspective?

2. What is the goal of this course, from the perspective of the participants (WIIFM)?

3. What is the goal of the course, from the perspective of the person commissioning it?

In light of these different expectations:

4. What will you call the course?

5. How will you describe the course in any publicity material and pre-course information?

6. How will you describe the course in your opening introduction?

2 Set up and set down

What happens before and after the learning event is more important than the event itself. Let us repeat that: what happens **before** the learning event – **the set up** – and what happens **after** – **the set down** – is more important than the learning event itself. Why? Because we need to judge learning events not by how enjoyable they are, but by how useful they are. The usefulness of a learning event hinges more on the preparation of, and the follow-up to, that learning event than on the event itself. Described below are some things you can do to set up and set down.

Set up

- ○ Get participants to commit to work-based projects which will ensure that the learning is put into action immediately after the course.
- ○ Make the training programme part of a bigger process, not just a stand-alone.
- ○ Space out the learning opportunities.
- ○ Agree specific business projects up-front (before the training) with the learners and the learners' manager(s), so that they know in advance what they need to go back and achieve.
- ○ Link rewards to the transfer of learning.

Set down

- ○ Follow up evaluation interviews with the learners' manager(s).
- ○ Provide on-the-job coaching opportunities.
- ○ Send each participant an audiotape filled with reminders and reinforcers – in a concert review format, if appropriate (see Tool 44, 'Music').
- ○ Divide the group into learning buddies who will coach each other at regular, agreed intervals.
- ○ Send a series of reinforcing 'trickle tips' and reminders by e-mail.
- ○ Create and circulate a video of people who are successfully applying the learning.
- ○ Use the organization's intranet to capture success stories and fresh application ideas.
- ○ Create an online bulletin board.
- ○ Create a physical bulletin board near heavily travelled areas, containing pictures of successful learners, reminders, tips, a 'help yourself' pocket of cards containing job aids or checklists, and a graffiti section where people can add their own stories, comments and pictures.
- ○ Place reinforcing messages on posters and peripherals where people can't fail to see them (in the lift, the mirrors in the toilet, in the canteen,

by entrance and exit doors, next to clocks, in stairwells, in pay envelopes, on vending machines or along corridors as mobiles or displays). Don't leave them up for ever – keep changing the messages to reflect what's just been learned.

○ Hold picnic lunches or breakfasts during which learners share stories.

○ Interview learners and ask them about their experiences of applying the learning. Ask what else you could have done in the training that would have made the learning easier to transfer. Take the lessons back into your design.

○ Ask the learners to train or coach others who didn't attend the training event.

○ Ask previous participants to come along and talk to the current group of learners – have them give a five-minute presentation on how they have successfully applied the learning.

○ Require each participant to write a short report summarizing how they successfully applied the learning. Collate these together and send all participants a copy.

○ Develop managers in the skills of supporting, coaching and reinforcing the learning back on the job. Make this a priority in your management development strategy.

Activity: Set up and set down

Identify a particular learning event for which you are responsible.

1. What do you currently do by way of set up and set down?

2. If you were determined to make this your best learning event ever, what would you do to enhance the set up and set down?

3. Given the resources of time and money you actually have available, what can you realistically to do by way of set up and set down?

3 Real projects

It's budget time at Bloggs's Widgets. The members of the board know they are facing intense competition. Rival firm, Wonder Widgets, is just down the road, and the newly launched Widgets.com is selling at knock-down prices.

The board are assembled to receive a number of investment proposals. First is the manufacturing director. She wants to buy a smart new widget machine which costs a cool £2m. She fires up her PowerPoint presentation and explains to the board the historical costs of their existing machines, and the return the company has already received on that investment. She then goes on to demonstrate the return on the proposed investment in the new machine. The details are a little tricky, but the headline figure is this: after three years the machine will pay for itself, and will then generate pure profit for the next seven years of its expected working life. The board are impressed, but have other proposals to listen to before making a decision.

Next is the sales and marketing director. He wants to invest £200 000 in a new Internet-based promotion campaign. The company has never done anything like this before but, using figures produced from comparable organizations, he demonstrates that for every £1 the company spends on the campaign it can expect to generate an additional £20 in revenue. Again, the board is impressed.

The final proposal today is from you – the learning and development manager. You want a mere £20 000 for a new leadership programme. You remind the board of their commitment to learning and development in the corporate plan and reiterate the importance of leadership in a modern company. But before you have finished making your case, the CEO interrupts with a question: 'What is the expected financial return on this proposed investment of £20 000?'

You come out with the usual arguments: it's very difficult to evaluate the impact of training on business performance because so many other factors play a part; training is an investment for the long term; and so on. But you don't have a direct answer to the question. You know that the board is not convinced and you leave the meeting with your tail between your legs. Later that day you hear that manufacturing got their £2m, marketing got their £200 000 and you are allocated just £10 000. You are heard to mutter darkly about the company's lack of vision.

Of course, you are wrong and the board is absolutely right. It would be quite irresponsible of the board to make any investment decision without some idea of the projected return on that investment. Imagine how you'd feel if you discovered that the manufacturing director had been allowed to buy a new machine on a whim, with no idea of the measurable benefit to the business. I hope you'd feel outraged.

Investment in training is in the same category of any other business investment – or at least it should be. Unless you can measure the business benefit, you shouldn't do it. But everyone knows how difficult it is to measure the impact of training on business performance. What can be done?

To answer this question you have to rethink the way you go about organizing training and learning events. All too often, the sequence is like this: the training department conducts some kind of training needs analysis; training courses are designed around behavioural objectives; there is some attempt at evaluation of training. It's very rare indeed for the evaluation to demonstrate that training has made any convincing contribution to business results.

Yet, training first and evaluating second is putting the cart before the horse. It is much more effective to identify measurable, worthwhile improvements in business results first, and then devise a training and development programme specifically to achieve them.

In order to pinpoint measurable, worthwhile improvements in business you have to identify the projects which the participants on your learning event are committed to doing after the training. The focus of attention must be on the projects – the training is there to ensure that the people have the knowledge, skills and attitudes needed to complete them.

Any kind of training and development can be project-based, and some kinds of development lend themselves to it. Instead of running a course on quality improvement, ask participants to identify specific quality improvement projects which will have a measurable result on the business – for example, reducing scrap and rework by 50 per cent, or speeding up cycle time by 20 per cent. Once the projects are clear, you can design a learning event to enable participants to achieve them.

"Aha!' I hear you say. 'It's easy when it comes to a topic such as quality improvement, where we already have the metrics in place to measure it. What about something that is important, but not easily measurable, like leadership?' There are two ways of measuring the business impact of leadership training – the direct method and the indirect method. Let's return to Bloggs's Widgets.

First, let's look at the direct way. Before putting your proposal to the board of Bloggs's Widgets, talk to each of the prospective participants on your leadership course individually. Ask them to identify a specific business improvement they would like to bring about in the company. It doesn't have to be anything new – indeed, many of them will already have 'projects' in mind, such as increasing sales, improving quality, preparing management accounts more accurately and so on. Then use your facilitation skills to help each manager put some kind of financial benefit on the project which they have identified. This will be easier in some cases than in others, but you don't need a detailed costing – just an idea of whether the project will benefit the company to the tune of £5000 rather than, say, £1000 or £10 000.

Once you have talked to each of the prospective participants, you design a leadership course which will help them achieve these projects and take your proposal to the board. You can then say, with some confidence, that this course will cost £20 000, but will enable the people who participate to generate measurable benefits to the company of £40 000 in the first year alone (or whatever figures you've come up with from talking to the prospective participants).

The advantage of this direct approach is that you link the training directly to specific projects. The drawback (and it is a drawback which applies to most methods of investment appraisal) is that it can take some time for the results to come through. For this reason, you might like to combine this direct method with the indirect method, which provides much more rapid results. This is how it works.

Before they attend your training programme, get the participants to engage in some kind of 360-degree feedback activity, which measures their current leadership behaviours. The 'project', for each of the participants, is to improve their scores on the leadership questionnaire when the feedback activity is repeated a few weeks after the course. The beauty of this approach is that, because the focus of attention is on changing leadership behaviours, rather than on the training course, you can use a whole raft of development activities to support the project. Coaching, mentoring, job shadowing and visits can all be slotted into place alongside course-based training in the service of the key project goal – to change leadership behaviours as measured by your 360-degree questionnaire.

So if the project is to improve scores on a questionnaire, what's the business benefit? What's the return on the investment? This is a separate discussion you need to have with the board, your chief executive or whoever is responsible for approving the investment in this leadership training. What value do the top management in your company put on good leadership? What's it worth to the company to have an outstanding leader in place of an average one?

Some companies will find this question easier to answer than others. If your company has some kind of competency-based reward system, then you automatically have a system for measuring what different levels of skill are worth to the company. Even if you don't have such a system, a mere comparison of salary figures should give you a rough idea.

To some extent, the figures you agree will be rather notional, but that's OK. Even when it comes to an investment appraisal of a piece of new machinery, many assumptions are made. Your manufacturing director doesn't really know whether the widge-o-matic machine will have a useful life of ten years, as opposed to five or 20, but it's important to have the discussion all the same. Investment appraisal is not an exact science, but it's better than nothing.

Even if you find it hard to place a monetary value on increasing business skills, the important thing (as Einstein once said) is not to stop questioning. I'm not pretending it is easy to assign financial benefits to the value of increasing leadership skills, I am saying that there are huge merits in posing the question – even if you only get some fairly rough and ready answers.

If the figures you put on the value of improved leadership skills turn out to be slightly inaccurate, this approach still has two enormous advantages over just running a training course and hoping for the best. First, participants come to your training course with clear goals. Not only will they be more attentive on the course, but they will apply the learning as soon as it finishes. This ensures that the learning is firmly embedded in long-term memory. Second, by engaging your CEO and board in a discussion about the business benefit of any training programme you provide, you are enhancing the credibility of your role in the organization. Whatever language is spoken throughout the rest of your organization, the language best understood by your board is the language of finance. Project-based training explains the benefits of training in a language the board can understand. And if this enhances your personal credibility in their eyes, that's not a bad thing either, is it?

Activity: Real projects

Choose a learning event you are currently responsible for.

1. What is the objective of the event?

2. How do you currently measure the effectiveness of the event?

3. How do you feel about the way the effectiveness of the event is currently measured?

4. In an ideal world what would you like the participants to do as a result of attending this learning event?

5. How could you turn this into a specific project with measurable results?

4 Real-life learning activities

There is a considerable body of research showing that the closer a learning activity resembles the real-life task, the greater the transfer of learning. In other words, if you train people to lead selection interviews by providing training in listening and questioning skills, this will be less effective than providing training which involves role-playing the kind of selection interviews these people will be carrying out in real life.

This research makes lots of sense. Think about learning a language. Simply learning grammar and vocabulary is going to be less effective than practising useful everyday phrases in realistic situations – booking a hotel room or ordering a meal, for example. Better still would be to actually visit the country where the language is spoken and practise in real life. Best of all, of course, would be to do all three!

All too often on training courses and other learning events we use examples which are one step removed from the participants' own experiences and needs. It is much better to use examples and activities which relate directly to the participants' experience and needs. Better still is to use examples and activities which are real for the participants.

Let's say you are running an event on facilitating meetings. Chances are you will do some kind of role-play. One option is to devise a case study and get the participants to role-play it. This has several drawbacks. First, you have to spend the time researching and devising a case study which all the participants can relate to. Second, because it is a case study you have written, it isn't real for the participants. A better approach is to get the participants to devise a scenario, based on a real meeting which has happened or which is about to happen. This will be much more relevant for the participants, and hence more fruitful for learning. Even better would be to get the participants to do a real meeting as part of the learning event. If you can't get the real participants to come to the training venue to take part in the meeting, you could have a telephone or even a video conference. If this sounds like a blurring of the boundary between training and real-time coaching, it is!

Here are some other examples of ways you can introduce real activities into different kinds of learning event.

Topic	Traditional approach	Brain-friendly approach
Health and safety	Lecture people about the company's policy.	Send people out into the factory to spot hazards and interview workers. Get them to write their own policy and then compare it with that of the company.
Coaching skills	Give a theoretical framework for coaching and do a few role-plays.	Choose a skill and get the experts to coach the learners. What did the experts do when they were coaching well? Now get everyone to go back into the office/factory and coach a real team member. Come back to the training room to debrief.
Computer training	Go through the manual step-by-step.	Get individuals to complete a real-life process relevant to them, with support and coaching from tutor and other participants.
Customer care	Lecture people on what they need to do to deliver customer care.	Give people a telephone, then have them ring up real customers to ask them what they want and how it compares to what they currently get.
Organizational change	Lecture people about the latest guru's model of change.	Give people a project to interview co-workers and find out what it would take to get them to change.
How brains work	Show people diagrams of the brain and talk to them about it.	Get people to *be* a brain – have small groups represent the different parts of the brain and interact with each other.
Training needs analysis	Do a TNA, do the training and then try to evaluate it afterwards. Give up because evaluation of training is too hard.	Identify specific business-focused projects for people to do – create learning events to equip them with the skills to deliver the projects. Measure the success of the training by the completion of the projects.

Activity: Real-life learning activities

Complete the following table. In the first column list at least four training courses which you are involved in. In the second column, list typical training activities. In the third column list possible real-life learning activities. Don't be constrained by what the company culture allows – what would you do if you were really passionate about creating extraordinary learning experiences?

Topic	Traditional approach	Brain-friendly approach

5 Rave review sessions

Remember, learning is the strengthening of connections between neurons – brain cells. The more often you repeat the learning, the stronger the connections become. Create plenty of opportunities to repeat and rehearse learning throughout the learning event. In fact, you've probably already noticed that concepts and ideas in one part of this manual are repeated elsewhere. That's a deliberate strategy – repetition is a brain-friendly way to learn.

Build plenty of review sessions throughout your learning event. Here are some ideas:

Thirteen rave review ideas

- ○ Throw a beanbag to a participant. They catch it and say one thing they've learnt so far. Then they throw the beanbag to the next person until everyone has had a go.
- ○ Everyone stands up, finds a partner and takes exactly two minutes to tell them everything they've learned so far. Repeat with another partner for two minutes.
- ○ In pairs or groups, participants prepare a Mind Map® of everything they've learned.
- ○ Small groups of participants prepare and perform a play, mime, rap or song which sums up the learning.
- ○ Put on some suitable music and talk through the main learning points in time to the music.
- ○ Put on some suitable music and show the participants some images or flipcharts which sum up the main learning points.
- ○ Ask the participants to speed-read the handouts/course manual.
- ○ Ask the participants to wander around the room scanning/reading the learning materials displayed.
- ○ Do a guided imagery exercise.
- ○ Create a gesture or movement which sums up the learning. Ask each participant in turn to create their own movement and describe the learning it encapsulates.
- ○ Divide the participants into pairs, A and B. Person B pretends to know nothing and person A teaches them everything they have learned so far. Have them swap roles.
- ○ Ask small groups of participants to design and deliver a short session for the groups.
- ○ Each participant writes and sends (then and there) an e-mail to their manager/team explaining what they have learned and what they will do with the learning.

Activity: Rave review sessions

Choose one of the review methods listed above. Use it *right now* to review everything you have learnt from this pack so far.

6 A warm welcome pack

The aim of this tool is to begin to create an appropriate state in the learners before they even arrive. Here are some ideas of what to include in your welcome pack:

- ❍ the big picture – maybe as a colourful Mind Map®
- ❍ advice on how to get the most from the event
- ❍ a summary of the difference this could make to their lives – and help in creating really compelling learning goals for themselves
- ❍ interesting 'snippets' or 'tasters' of the forthcoming material
- ❍ a quiz about the content
- ❍ glowing testimonials from previous participants
- ❍ useful things they can do before the course
- ❍ an audio- or video-cassette
- ❍ guided reading
- ❍ guidance on what to bring, what to wear and what to expect
- ❍ something about what the participants will have in common
- ❍ some useful and relevant websites.

Make this as 'human' as you can – steer away from the traditional 'joining instructions' approach which can feel rather impersonal. Put some passion into your language.

Activity: The ultimate welcome pack

Using the course you are focusing on, design the ultimate 'welcome pack'. What would create the state you want before the course even begins?

7 Energizing endings

Endings are important. If people have had a wonderful time, learned a great deal and made some good friends, it's natural for them to feel somewhat emotional towards the end of the event – perhaps excited, perhaps a little sad, close to the group, and determined to put their learning into practice.

A good ending needs four things:

○ emotional impact
○ integration of material
○ future pacing (transfer of learning)
○ a sense of closure.

Here are several ideas to incorporate into your endings.

Multisensory integration performance

Split the participants into groups of 3–5 and give them the challenge of designing and then performing something that encapsulates their learning. They could choose to:

○ draw a colourful picture or Mind Map®
○ create a rap, jingle or song (and, possibly, an accompanying dance too)
○ tell a metaphorical story
○ act out a short playlet or skit
○ create a physical memento – a 3D icon, sculpture, or job aid.

Guided visualization/mental rehearsal

Lead the participants through a closed-eye exercise in which they relax whilst rehearsing the behaviours and seeing, hearing and feeling themselves successfully achieving their goals.

Check out

This can be structured or unstructured, as appropriate. Have the group stand or sit in a circle and express whatever they want about the learning, about themselves, about each other and about what the event has meant to them. You could display trigger questions visually. If the group has developed a true intimacy, suggest a group hug or huddle as people express these parting thoughts.

Concert review

You, or somebody else, could do a final concert review (see Tool 44, 'Music').

Ball throw

Get the group to throw a soft ball around and commit, when they catch it, to their actions on returning to work – for example, 'The three things I'm going to do on Monday are . . .' There are endless variations on this theme.

Video commitments

An even more powerful technique is to ask each participant to stand up and present their vision, commitments or credo to a videocamera. Keep the videos and send them to the participants six weeks later, as a reminder.

Buddy pairs – commitments

Have the group pair up with a buddy to action commitments, and create a plan for how they will support each other back at work.

Personal goodbye and feedback

Give the group some time to wander round just saying what they want to say to each other. You could do this in an entirely unstructured way or, if you prefer, provide some structure. Ask each person to give every other person some positive feedback by completing the sentence 'The gift I see in you is . . .'. Variations on this theme include having people write the feedback on a 'flipchart poncho' that individuals have made and are wearing, or to write the feedback on a slip of paper and place it in the person's left shoe. (It's extraordinary how many seemingly 'tough', no-nonsense managers we meet who are demonstrably moved by this exercise, and keep their bits of paper for years!)

Repetition of course rituals

Close on some ritual that the participants are already familiar with – for example, brain gym, handclaps or anchored musical themes.

Inspiring quotes

Wish the group every success, acknowledge their achievements, and perhaps finish with one of your favourite, inspirational quotations. For example,

'Vision without Action is just dreaming.
Action without Vision just passes the time.
Vision – plus Action – can change the world.'
(Joel Barker)

Activity: Design your ending

Using your own ideas and the suggestions above, design an ending for your learning event that will achieve the four aims of:

- ○ emotional impact
- ○ integration of material
- ○ future pacing (transfer of learning)
- ○ a sense of closure.

Tools for facilitating creation

8 Mindblowing Mind Maps®

Invented in the late 1960s by Tony Buzan,[16] Mind Maps® are now used worldwide by millions of people – from the very young to the very old – whenever they wish to use their minds more effectively.

What is a Mind Map®?

A Mind Map® is a powerful graphic technique which provides a universal key to unlock the potential of the brain. It harnesses the full range of cortical skills – word, image, number, logic, rhythm, colour and spatial awareness – in a single, uniquely powerful manner. In so doing, it gives you the freedom to roam the infinite expanses of your brain. The Mind Map® can be applied to every aspect of life where improved learning and clearer thinking will enhance human performance.

Similar to a road map, a Mind Map® will:

- give you an overview of a large subject/area
- enable you to plan routes/make choices and let you know where you are going and where you have been
- gather and hold large amounts of data for you
- encourage problem-solving by showing you new creative pathways
- be enjoyable to look at, read, muse over and remember
- attract and hold your eye/brain
- let you see the whole picture *and* the details at the same time.

A Mind Map® makes learning, work and thinking enjoyable!

The table on page 93 was taken from the Mind Map® website, which you can find at <www.buzancentres.com>.

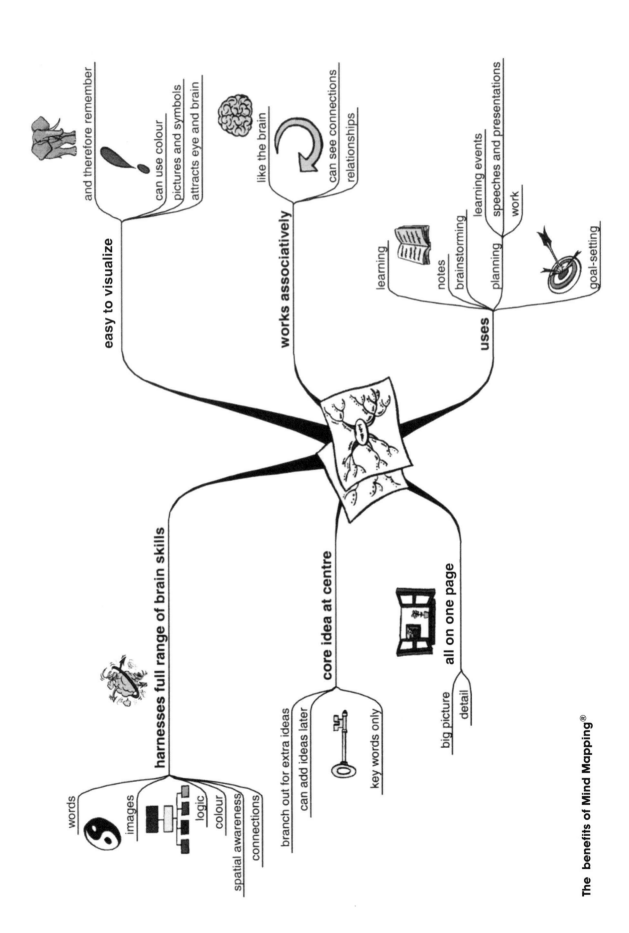

The benefits of Mind Mapping®

Uses	Benefits
Learning	Reduce those 'tons of work'. Feel good about study, revision and exams. Have confidence in your learning abilities.
Overviewing	See the whole picture, the global view, at once. Understand the links and connections.
Concentrating	Focus on the task for better results. Using all of your cortical skills attracts your attention.
Memorising	Easy recall. 'See' the information in your mind's eye.
Organising	Be on top of all of the details for parties, holidays, projects or any other subject.
Presenting	Speeches are clear, relaxed and alive. You can be at your best.
Communicating	In all forms with clarity and conciseness.
Planning	Orchestrate all details and aspects – from beginning to end – on one piece of paper.
Meetings	From planning to agenda, to chairing, to taking the minutes . . . the jobs are completed with speed and efficiency.
Training	From preparation to presentation they make the job easier and much faster .
Thinking	Having a method to analyse thoughts – almost a 'way-station' for them.
Negotiating	All the issues, your position and manoeuvrability in one sheet.
Brain Blooming	The new brain-storming in which more thoughts are generated and appropriately assessed.

We make substantial use of the great Mind Mapping® software tool 'MindManager'. You can download a free trial of this user-friendly, intuitive, software by visiting <www.mindmanager.co.uk>.

Activity: Mind Map® your design

Mind Map® a course you are designing. Your aim should be that, once the Mind Map® is complete, you can throw away all your other notes and session plans, and facilitate the event just using the Mind Map® as an *aide-mémoire*.

9 Contracting for success

Groups very quickly begin to establish psychological 'norms': how we behave here; what is acceptable and what is not; how we treat each other; how hard we work; what kind of humour is appropriate and so on. As this is a phenomenon that happens anyway, we can use it as an opportunity to create the most conducive learning environment.

Remember, learning is something you do with people, not for them. 'Contract' with the participants – agree explicitly how you are jointly going to create the most productive learning environment. This sets the 'groundrules' and establishes a set of behavioural norms that this particular group would find most helpful in maximizing their learning.

Useful questions for a contracting session are:

- ○ What do you want/expect from each other to enhance learning?
- ○ What do you want/expect from the facilitator to enhance learning?
- ○ What can you do to enhance learning?
- ○ What housekeeping rules do we need to agree – punctuality, use of mobile phones, confidentiality, and so on?

Participants can discuss these questions in small groups and then feed them back in a plenary discussion. You and the participants then agree a written contract.

It's generally best to do contracting towards the beginning of an event, but not right at the start. People need some time to get used to each other and to you before they can be clear about how they want the rest of the event to run. We like to do contracting just before or just after the first refreshment break of the event.

In our experience, a well-facilitated contract overcomes nearly all the problems caused by so-called 'difficult delegates' and it also gives a powerful message about who should be taking responsibility for both behaviour and learning.

Display the contract in a visible place so that everybody can keep referring back to it.

10 Keep the ball in the learner's court

One of the principles of brain-friendly learning is to keep the ball in the learner's court as much as possible – aim for about 70 per cent of the time. Here are some ideas.

Traditional learning	Brain-friendly learning
Trainer writes case studies and asks participants to discuss them.	Participants work in groups to write case studies. Each group passes its case study on to the next group to work on.
Trainer explains a complicated process using diagrams and charts.	Participants map out the process themselves using huge rolls of paper or physical objects.
Trainer explains a complicated process using diagrams and charts.	Participants physically act out/demonstrate the process.
Trainer hands out written information and talks it through.	Divide participants into groups. Give each group a chunk of the written information and ask them to read it and become an expert. Then other groups send visitors to this group to ask questions of the experts.
Trainer explains company policy on topic X.	Give participants an opportunity to get to grips with the topic, then ask them to write a policy and compare it with the company policy. For example, let them wander round the factory looking for hazards and then write a health and safety policy.
Trainer tells participants how important concept Y is.	Design a participative activity which demonstrates how important concept Y is. For example, instead of talking about how important it is to listen carefully to customers, set up an activity where participants have an experience of not being listened to, so they know what it feels like!
Trainer explains a concept or model.	Give participants relevant information and ask them to design a model or concept.

Activity: Spot the ball

Take an existing training programme. Analyse the percentage of time which is trainer input, as opposed to learner activity. How can you put the ball back in the learner's court?

11 Creation not consumption

Learning is about the creation of value, not just the consumption of information. This is a practical, as well as a philosophical, point. How can you encourage participants to create, rather than consume? Here are some ways of getting participants to create learning materials.

- ○ Have lots of coloured pens available and encourage doodling, Mind Mapping® and note-taking.
- ○ Encourage participants to record learning on flipcharts and display these throughout the learning event.
- ○ Have a pinboard on which participants can pose questions and offer answers to each other.
- ○ Use a digital camera to record key moments from the learning event and display photographs on the walls or through a data projector.
- ○ Identify a learning theme for the event and give participants suitable scrap materials with which to create an appropriate learning environment.
- ○ Encourage participants to create *aide mémoires* of the learning event and have them laminated for longer life.
- ○ When an event occurs more than once, ask participants to create the learning materials – handout, posters and so on – for the next run of the event.
- ○ Get participants to devise learning materials and put them on a CD or the company intranet.

Activity: Create – don't just consume!

Get yourself a set of fine tipped felt-tip pens and a large sheet of paper. Give yourself exactly five minutes to doodle on the subject 'Learning is creation, not consumption'. Doodle. Sketch. Write down words as they occur to you. Don't worry about what's coming out – allow your unconscious mind to lead you where it will. You don't have to show anyone else the finished product – you are doing this to please yourself. If the idea of doodling like this is alien to you, remember it's only five minutes out of your life! Go on, do it and have fun!

When the five minutes is up, stop! Now take a look at what you've done. What insights are there? How could you adapt this technique for your next learning event?

12 The power of questions

'The important thing is not to stop questioning.'
(Albert Einstein)

'The wise man doesn't give the right answers, he poses the right questions.'
(Claude Levi-Strauss)

'Good questions outrank easy answers.'
(Paul Samuelson)

'It is better to know some of the questions than all of the answers.'
(James Thurber)

A facilitator of brain-friendly learning will ask lots of questions. Perhaps one of the earliest exponents of brain-friendly learning was Leonardo da Vinci. He excelled as an architect, botanist, chef, engineer, inventor, geologist, mathematician, musician, painter, philosopher and physicist. And he had an insatiable curiosity. His notebooks record that he would often begin the day by brainstorming a hundred questions. One of his biographers described him as 'undoubtedly the most curious man who ever lived' – someone who 'wouldn't take yes for an answer'.

How can you develop this kind of insatiable inquisitiveness and curiosity in your participants? Ask lots of questions! Not just 'What do you know about the company's health and safety policy?' but also:

- ❍ 'What would it be like if we had no health and safety policy?'
- ❍ 'Who would like to work in a company that had a health and safety record of a Victorian coal mine?'
- ❍ 'If you really wanted to create a dangerous work environment, what would you do?'

Activity: Questions, questions

Identify a topic for which you are designing a learning event.

- ❍ Step one
  Brainstorm at least 28 questions about this topic. Yes, 28! Keep going until you have 28 questions, however banal or seemingly irrelevant.

- ❍ Step two
  Have you got at least 28? Good! If not, go back to step one until you have!
  Once you've got 28, choose the six most interesting and write them here. A bit of rephrasing is allowed . . .

- ○ Step three
  Now design a learning event which enables participants to pose and answer those six questions.

- ○ Step four
  Now design a learning event which enables participants to pose and answer their own questions about this topic.

Do I hear some of you asking, 'Why 28 questions?' It's good to be curious, and we'll not give you an answer straightaway for reasons which will become apparent as you read on.

'The riddle does not exist. If a question can be put at all, then it can also be answered.'
(Ludwig Wittgenstein)

When a participant on a training course asks a question it's very tempting to give them an answer – but don't! If you supply the answer, it stops them learning.

Example: 'What happens in Word when I press F7?'

- ○ Possible answer 1): 'It activates the spellchecker'.
- ○ Possible answer 2): 'Why don't you try it?
- ○ Possible answer 3): 'It causes the computer to self-destruct!'

A likely response to answer number 3 is: 'No, I think it activates the spellchecker.' To which the natural rejoinder is: 'Well, if you knew, why did you ask me?'

This mode of thinking pervades in all sorts of scenarios. For example:

'My mother is old and frail – what should I do?'
'Have her put down?'
'No! I was thinking of getting her a home help.'
'So, why are you asking me?'

If someone frames a question they have almost certainly some idea of the answer. The role of the facilitator is to help them bring this and the embedded criteria they are using to decide on it, to the surface. It is reflecting on these criteria that provides the real value of questions, and the resultant insights. So, the next time someone on a course asks you a question:

1 Don't answer.
2 Ask them what they think the answer is.
3 If they say 'I don't know', ask them to guess.

13 Associative learning

All learning is associative; we learn new concepts, ideas and skills by associating them with existing learning.

The word *springle* probably means nothing to you. If I tell you that it is a piece of jewellery you then associate the word, springle, with jewellery and learning takes place. If I tell you that it is a piece of jewellery shaped like a coil and worn around your wrist you can make associations with the words spring and bangle and remember the word for ever. Association can be particularly useful when learning foreign languages and technical material.

How can we use the concept of associative learning to make learning easier?

1 **Disseminate pre-course information.**
   By sending participants information in advance about the learning event, you not only begin to put them in a good learning state, but also give them an overall picture of the course.

2 **Elicit existing learning.**
   If you want to associate new learning with existing learning, it can help to find out what the learners already know. We usually begin our sessions on how the brain works by asking participants to brainstorm everything they currently know about the brain. This brings to the front of their mind an existing framework on which to hang new learning.

3 **Give a big picture overview.**
   At the start of a learning event, give the participants an overview of the main topics to be covered.

4 **Use relevant metaphors.**
   In the movie *The Full Monty*, a group of unemployed steelworkers in Sheffield decide to become male strippers. As part of their striptease routine they are trying to learn a particularly tricky dance sequence. At one point their teacher explains that it is just like a particular passing movement in a game of football. Suddenly, they've all got it. Explaining new learning in terms of a metaphor they can all relate to makes it very easy. There's more on metaphors in 'Tools for making it rich and multisensory'.

How existing learning can hamper new learning

'The doctor's son greeted his father.' Now answer this question quickly – what profession is the father?

Most people's immediate answer to this question is 'A doctor, of course', rather than the correct answer, which is that it's impossible to tell. All you know is that this boy has a mother or a father who is a doctor, but you don't know which. So why do most people spontaneously answer that the father is the doctor? Because most people have a mental picture that doctors are often men, which is reinforced by the masculine words used in the sentence (son, father), which in turn encourage association with further male images.

Sometimes existing learning can obstruct new learning. Let's say you are leading a training session on performance appraisal. In the past, this has been carried out in your company in a rather autocratic way, with the manager very much sitting in judgement on the subordinate. You are trying to promote a model of appraisal which is more developmental and empowering.

What existing learning do your participants already have about appraisal? They may associate it with the company's existing scheme. They may associate it with experiences they've had at other companies – good and bad. They many associate it with being back at school and being hauled into the headteacher's office for a telling off. These current associations may not all be very helpful with regard to the new learning you wish to promote.

One useful technique here is to elicit the existing learning with the explicit purpose of turning it around. For example, you could ask participants to design the very *worst* appraisal system they possibly could, based on their experience, and, having done that, use this data to design the very *best* appraisal system they possibly could.

Activity: Relating new learning to existing learning

Think about a learning event you will be facilitating. How can you use these techniques to relate new learning to existing learning?

Activity: Friends, Romans . . .

Have you ever wondered how the Ancient Romans and Greeks used to make long speeches without written notes or an autocue? OK, probably not, but maybe you should, because they used a very interesting method based on the power of associative learning. They called it the method of loci. This is what they did. First, they imagined a series of locations that were very familiar – the inside of their villa, or a familiar part of the city perhaps. Then they associated each part of their speech with a particular location. Here's an example:

Speech	Location	Association
Friends, Romans and countrymen …	Entrance hall	I often welcome my friends at the entrance hall.
lend me your ears.	Reception room	I have two large jugs in my reception room that look just like ears.
I come to bury Caesar not to praise him	Back garden	My old pet dog is buried in the garden – I'd like to put Caesar there too.

As the orator imagines himself wandering through his house, he is prompted to think of the next line of his speech.

Use this method to remember your opening lines of welcome at the next learning event you are hosting.

14 Crystal-clear instructions

As a facilitator of learning, you often have to give people instructions – to form groups of a certain size, to take a break, to come back after the break, to stand up, to sit down, to turn to page 94 of the training manual and so on. How can you give these instructions in the most effective way? Here are some tips.

○ **Give instructions rather than ask questions.**
'Please stand up now' works better than 'Would you mind standing up now?'.

○ **Shorter is better than longer.**
'Please stand up now' works better than 'Here's what I'd like you to do. I'd like you to stand up now, if it's not too much trouble, and, er, when you're standing up, well, just stand and then I'll explain what you are going to be doing next – OK? So stand up as soon as you're ready.'

○ **Make your voice tone, body language and gesture consistent with your spoken message.**
Say 'please stand up now' in a confident tone of voice, and use your arms and hands to make a 'please stand up now' kind of gesture. (This is much harder to explain in words than it is to do – imagine you had to mime to someone the instruction 'please stand up now' and you'll have the right kind of gesture.)

○ **Use consistent phrases, voice tone and gestures for the same instruction.**
For example, whenever you want people to refer to the course manual, use a consistent voice tone, cadence and gesture as you say, 'Please grab your manuals and turn to page ... 94'. Pausing after the word 'page' will help people remember which page to turn to.

   When you use consistent phrases, voice tone and gestures you create an anchor (see 'Tools for managing state' for more on anchors). Once the anchor is established, you need only say 'Please grab your manuals . . .' to have the full attention of your participants.

○ **Use a trigger to get participants' attention after a practical activity.**
You can either use a consistent phrase and voice tone which works for you, or you can use some kind of musical instrument. Little bells or chimes work well. One trainer we know has a wooden whistle which sounds like an American steam train.

Activity: Precise instructions

The next time you lead a learning event, pay particular attention to the way in which you give instructions. Do you tend to ask questions? Are your instructions unnecessarily long or even rambling? Are you conveying a consistent message with your words, voice tone, body language and gestures?

In the spaces below, list the precise words and specify the body language you will use to:

1. put people into pairs

2. put people into groups of four

3. get people on their feet

4. get people to pay attention to you after activities

5. tell people to go for a break

6. get people to return from a break

7. get people to stand up

8. get people to sit on each other's laps in a circle

Now practise the words and the accompanying body language and gestures until you are completely comfortable with them and they become natural.

15 First and last gets remembered

Activity: Memory test

Read this list of items once and remember as many as you can.

- ○ Apple
- ○ Gate
- ○ Forceps
- ○ Fish
- ○ Glow
- ○ Bicycle
- ○ Table
- ○ Orgasm
- ○ Plate
- ○ Pen
- ○ Car

Now cover the list with a sheet of paper and answer these questions:

1. What was the first word on the list?

2. What was the last word on the list?

3. What other words can you remember?

Most people tend to remember the first and last word on the list. This phenomenon is known as primacy and recency. In most learning situations – whether reading random words on a list or participating in a training course – you will tend to remember the first thing and the last thing. The first and the last learning points in any training session will tend to be remembered above those in the middle.

It follows that you can increase the learning on your courses simply by having more breaks. This means that you have more sessions and therefore more incidents of primacy and recency. Breaks are also beneficial because they allow people to move around, increase their oxygen and adrenaline levels, and generally get into a more productive learning state. They also give participants some downtime to process the information they have already absorbed. Exact timings will depend on the participants and the subject matter but, as a rough rule of thumb, organize learning in chunks of between 30 and 50 minutes, with short breaks in between each chunk.

Was 'orgasm' one of the other words you remembered from the list? In the same way that primacy and recency help learning, anything which is a little unusual or which has an emotional content is more easily remembered. The success of the board game *Trivial Pursuit* is a testament to human beings' ability to remember anything which is a little unusual or, frankly, silly.

Activity: First and last gets remembered

Many trainers quite properly give plenty of thought to the way they begin a session on a training course. But it is less common to pay quite as much attention to the endings of sessions. All too often they can degenerate into a rush towards the coffee cups rattling in the corridor outside. Yet the ending of a session is as important as the beginning so far as participants' learning is concerned.

Sketch out in the space below a brief outline of the sessions in a learning event for which you are responsible. Now pay close attention to the endings for each session. Write down how you will handle these endings, either by using a mini-activity (perhaps some kind of review session) or by scripting the words you will say. Is there a short story you can tell to make this bit of learning more memorable? Write your ideas down.

Sessions	Session endings
1	1
2	2
3	3
4	4
5	5
6	6

16 Chunking

In 1956 George Miller[20] published an article in *Psychological Review* that was to become a classic. Miller argues that people tend to learn most efficiently in units of seven, plus or minus two. Groups of seven appear throughout history (for example, the seven deadly sins, the seven wonders of the ancient world, seven brides for seven brothers) and telephone numbers which have more than seven digits are usually broken down into smaller chunks – 01535645519 is hard to handle, but 01535 645519 is more manageable.

More recently Nelson Cowan[21] has refined Miller's research to show that units of four (plus or minus two) are even more easily remembered than chunks of seven. The message is: if you want to convey complex information, break it into smaller chunks.

Let's say you gave people a checklist for a training venue like this:

- ❍ Clear signage so that people can find the venue
- ❍ Notice by door with name of training course
- ❍ Comfortable room temperature
- ❍ Adequate ventilation
- ❍ Adequate lighting
- ❍ Soundproofing
- ❍ Some natural daylight
- ❍ Comfortable chairs
- ❍ Seating layout appropriate to the event
- ❍ Water to drink
- ❍ Refreshments easily available
- ❍ Toilets nearby
- ❍ Enough space for the number of participants – as a rule of thumb, at least 4 sq m per person
- ❍ Appropriate audiovisual equipment – flipcharts, data projector, OHP, video player and TV, computers.

Remembering 14 different items is a bit of a challenge, but not if you chunk it down into groups like this:

Signage
- ❍ Clear signage so that people can find the venue
- ❍ Notice by door with name of training course.

Physical comfort
- ❍ Comfortable room temperature
- ❍ Adequate ventilation
- ❍ Adequate lighting
- ❍ Soundproofing

❍ Some natural daylight
❍ Comfortable chairs.

Layout
❍ Seating layout appropriate to the event
❍ Enough space for the number of participants – as a rule of thumb, at least 4 sq m per person.

Refreshments
❍ Water to drink
❍ Refreshments easily available
❍ Toilets nearby.

Equipment
❍ Appropriate audiovisual equipment – flipcharts, data projector, OHP, video player and TV, computers.

Instead of a long list, there are five main chunks, each of which consists of at most six items – much easier to deal with.

Activity: Brainstorm cluster

Brainstorm everything you would want the participants on your next course to be able to know or do at the end of it. Instead of brainstorming on to a blank sheet of paper, brainstorm on to a Post-it pad – one Post-it note for each item of your brainstorm. Continue until you have at least 20 items.

Spread out all the Post-its on a table top, and then begin to cluster them into groups of related items. When you think about this topic again, your mind will automatically focus first on the 'big chunks' – the clusters – allowing you to see and remember the big picture easily. As you then focus on each cluster, your mind will have 'filed' the detailed points using association.

17 Integration smorgasbord

Here are some more ideas for keeping the ball in the learner's court.

Coaching pairs

One partner is 'A', the other 'B'. Have them take it in turns to coach or 'teach' each other on the content of the session.

Heads and tails

Pairs toss a coin to see who is 'Heads' and who is 'Tails'. 'Tails' has to describe, to their partner, the obstacles to applying what has been learned in practice – the barriers, the difficulties, why it won't work. After listening to this, 'Heads' has to 'sell' the learning and do whatever it takes to help the other person overcome the challenges they might face. Then they reverse roles.

My mistake!

This is especially good for technical or IT training. Divide the participants into pairs. Have one partner deliberately put errors into the system. The other has to recover from, or correct, the error, and explain what they are doing and why. Then they reverse roles.

Create your own . . .

Have small groups create a colourful Mind Map®, pictogram, graphic, job aid, 3D icon, video film, cartoon, mnemonic, story, playlet, rap, jingle, dance or song about what they have just learned (and then perform or display these to whole group).

Cocktail questions

This is good just before a break. Write up a question or a statement you want participants to answer or complete, such as 'The most interesting thing about that last session for me was . . .' or 'One thing I'm definitely going to do on returning to work is . . .' (the variations on this are endless). Put some cocktail party music on. Everybody then stands up and, miming holding a cocktail glass in one hand, circulate round the room, answering the question or completing the statement.

Stump your buddy

In pairs, each participant asks their partner three challenging questions about the topic being explored. They then swap roles and repeat.

Hangman

Pairs of participants play hangman – a 'wrong' answer brings the 'noose' a little closer.

Create a peripheral

Have pairs or small groups make a peripheral about the session for the room – an object, a wall decoration, a mobile, a floor decoration or a tabletop display.

Recruit your colleagues

Have pairs or small groups create an attractive poster 'selling' the benefits of the workshop that they've just experienced. (These are great to actually use, too.)

Help your buddy

In pairs, participants spend time with each other helping to prepare for an upcoming test or skill assessment.

Team teaching

Give each small group the responsibility for teaching all its members to master some knowledge or a skill. You can provide suggestions, but the team is fully responsible for deciding how they will go about this in a way that achieves really positive results.

Walkie talkie

Give pairs a challenging question or issue to think through, and have them go for a walk whilst they explore it.

Research and present back

Ask pairs or small groups to research a topic and then present their findings to the whole group.

DYO quiz

Have groups design challenging questions covering any of the material on the course. They then pose these to a 'rival' group or team, in a game show-type format. The 'rules' are that the team asking the question must have a really good answer prepared, and that only 'fair' questions that will help people learn are admissible. There are many variations on this theme.

Integration activity design

Assign groups the task of 'reviewing' some aspect of the learning. They can design a game, an activity – anything that helps their colleagues to embed the material.

Debating teams

Give teams some time to prepare arguments from opposing sides of an issue, and then hold a formal debate.

Best and worst scavenger hunt

Give teams a finite amount of time to find the 'best' and 'worst' examples they can from inside or outside their own organization. (For example, if your course focuses on customer care, send them out to a nearby high street to find good and bad real-life examples.) Each team reports back with their findings.

Ideas scavenger hunt

At the end of a session, ask the learners to generate relevant, workable ideas that they could apply by looking in unexpected places. For example, after a session on continuous improvement, ask them to find three great ideas from today's newspaper, or a completely unrelated journal such as *Waste Management Monthly*. Or send them to a local business (from a different industry). Or send them for a 10-minute walk in the country, during which they are to identify three great ideas from nature that they could borrow and use in their own organization.

Collaborative pre-test

Have groups work together on completing a pre-test or knowledge self-assessment before new material is presented. Tell them to cheat like mad, using any resources they can. If there is a test at the end of the course, give them the 'final exam' right at the beginning.

Group brain

The whole group stands up and becomes a group brain – each person is an individual neuron. The facilitator makes a statement and throws a ball to somebody, who has 15 seconds to confer with the 'neuron' to the right or the left of them. The neuron responds, and throws the ball back to the facilitator, who then asks another question or makes another statement.

Mental rehearsal

Have learners mentally rehearse the way in which they will transfer or apply the learning in the future, including overcoming any associated obstacles, and feeling good during the process.

Active listening

If you are lecturing or presenting, ask the learners to do something definite whilst listening, such as creating a Mind Map® of the presentation topic or generating three useful questions to ask at the end.

Quiet reflection

Provide time for the learners to be alone or away from the group to reflect, rewrite their notes, formulate questions, or simply organize their thoughts about what they are learning.

Brain-friendly presentations

Make your presentation different by doing it in the style of a talk show, a news bulletin, a press conference (have learners 'planted' with questions), a story hour, a bingo game (with learners completing information on bingo cards), a crossword (with learners completing the crossword as new information emerges) or a demonstration of a process or system, using people as props.

Application news

Provide Post-its on each table, and a large board or wall. As the session progresses, ask people to write a 'headline' of how they could, or will, apply the learning back in the workplace – for example, 'John Smith reinvigorates team meetings by introducing giving out spot prizes for great ideas'. At the end of the session, ask the group to create a newspaper that acts as a summary of their planned actions.

Feedforward

Ask participants to prepare a three-minute evaluation of the learning – what worked well for them, what improvements they would recommend. This can double up as an integration and feedback piece.

Active reading

Instead of just asking people to 'read' some relevant text, encourage them to create something as they read – a Mind Map®, a plan of how they would teach it to somebody else, a mnemonic or flowchart.

Ask the experts

Have Post-it notes on the tables, and create a board or wall hanging entitled 'Ask the Experts'. At any time, a learner may write a question on a Post-it and attach it to the board. At regular intervals, pull these Post-its from the board, read them aloud, and ask for volunteers from the group to answer them.

Alternatively, distribute the Post-its so that each small group or table answers a different question from the one they posed. You can, of course, also choose to give your view – but let the group express their ideas first.

Concert review

The course material can be reviewed in auditory or visual forms (or both) whilst playing music. The review can take the form of a closed-eye exercise in which somebody runs through the material verbally or the group can rewatch a slide or PowerPoint presentation. Alternatively, invite the group to walk around the room reading material and peripherals displayed on the walls. Video can also be used to review the previous day's experience.

Problem-pose

Pose a real-life problem at the start of a session, and integrate the material by having small groups solve the problem, or suggest strategies.

Make it real!

Learners go off to carry out a real-life activity in the workplace, and then come back to discuss it.

Choose your own . . .

Ask the learners to choose how they can best integrate and embed the learning.

18 The Disney strategy

Designing a learning event which truly keeps the ball in the learner's court requires some creativity. How can you allow your creative energies to flow and still come up with something that will work with real participants?

This strategy came from observations made of Walt Disney and how he used different thought modes to do different things. Disney could move from being a Dreamer to a Realist or a Critic at will, depending on what the circumstances were. This is how you can do the same.

There are three distinct stages to the Disney creativity strategy.

1. Dreamer

In this stage, you freely associate to a topic. Your perception is widened and you start to explore without constructively assessing your exploration. Quite often, ideas emerge for no good reason, and they often seem unconnected to the original topic. This is the stage when the ideas 'pop' into your head **before** you start to evaluate and either accept or dismiss them.

2. Realist

This is a way of looking at and balancing the necessary resources to make the creative idea or dream a 'reality'. This is the time when the real world encroaches on the great idea. Can it be done?

3. Critic

This is the stage when you look critically at an idea and look for the weak points and the good points, and 'pick holes in it'. Here you freely evaluate the chances of success given the nature of the idea and the balance of available resources.

How to use the strategy

STEP 1

On the floor pick out three specific places where you can step, one for Dreamer, one for Realist and one for Critic.

STEP 2

Step into your Dreamer space and remember an occasion when you were highly creative. Close your eyes and try to recall as many details of that time as possible. Increase the number and intensity of pictures, sounds and feelings that you associate with this memory and make them all stronger. Try to relive the occasion in more detail than you did at the time. Step out and repeat the process in the Realist space (remembering a time when you were highly realistic) and the Critic space (remembering a time when you were very constructively critical).

STEP 3

Now repeat the whole, threefold process, making sure that you mentally experience strong feelings, pictures and any associated sound for each of the places and modes.

STEP 4

Take your problem and think about it **only** from the creative Dreamer position. Only be a creative person whilst contemplating the problem. Look for new ideas that may solve it. Note down the ideas that come.

STEP 5

Now take one of the ideas and go into the Realist position and think about the idea from that mode **only**.

STEP 6

Note any changes you may need to that idea as a result of going into the Realist space. Then take this new solution and go into the Critic position and consider it as a critic **only**.

STEP 7

Note any changes that need to be made as a result of evaluation from the Critic position and, again, take it to your creative/Dreamer position to check whether the idea still holds good there. Continue to cycle through all three positions making amendments until you are comfortable with the idea and solution in all three.

Activity: Disney strategy walkthrough

Use the Disney strategy to 'walk through' your final course design from each of the three perspectives.

Each one will give you powerful feedback and ideas to improve your plans. Write some notes here.

19 The flexible facilitator

Watch a group that meets regularly, and you can observe a definite pattern of development with stages of growth and maturity. These stages of development are observable in any work team, but they also become apparent during a group training event – especially one which is longer than a day or so. They are as follows:

- ○ Stage one: **Forming**
  (*Also called* **testing** *or* **ritual sniffing**!)
- ○ Stage two: **Storming**
  (*Also called* **infighting**)
- ○ Stage three: **Norming**
  (*Also called* **getting organized**)
- ○ Stage four: **Performing**
  (*Also called* **mature rapport**)

The table on page 118 shows the characteristic behaviours observed at each stage.

It is tempting to try to push groups through the first three stages because they are less productive, but teams (like individuals) need to grow to maturity. However, this does not mean that you have to wait years for groups to reach the performing stage – a group of skilled and motivated people can reach this level very quickly – but the process cannot be forced, and the stages cannot be 'skipped'. If they are, groups often behave in a way which is best described as 'pseudo-performing' where people try very hard to be businesslike, authentic and 'mature', but underlying tensions have not been dealt with and conflict never really surfaces.

Some researchers have noted that some groups go through two other stages:

DORMING
when groups have worked together for a long time and become complacent, or 'fat and happy'

MOURNING
the sadness experienced by group members when a group is split up at the end of a project or task

When new members join a group, there is often a slide back to the earlier stages of development, and the group temporarily ceases to be productive until the new person is fully integrated.

Your role as facilitator, then, is to help this process along. You need to adopt the most appropriate style and behaviour to help move the team on to the next stage in their development.

Activity: Facilitator style

Look at the following table, showing characteristic behaviours of groups at each stage.

Identify some specific actions the facilitator could take that would be appropriate at each stage and would also help accelerate the group's development to the next stage.

Stage	Characteristic behaviours in group	Appropriate facilitator style and strategies
Forming	◇ Testing and dependence on leader ◇ Polite and impersonal ◇ Concern for structure ('Who is in charge?') ◇ Silences. anxiety, suspicion or fear Guarded, hesitant behaviours – only 'safe' topics get discussed ◇ Complaints about environment ◇ Intellectualizing and reluctance to express feelings ◇ Minimal work accomplishment	
Storming	◇ Infighting and conflict – often noisy ◇ Formation of sub groups ◇ Establishment of pecking order ◇ Feelings of getting nowhere and being stuck ◇ Rebellion or challenges to the leader ◇ Establishing unrealistic goals ◇ Opting out by individuals ◇ Disunity, jealousy and turf issues ◇ Minimal work accomplishment	
Norming	◇ Getting organized and clarifying roles ◇ Increase in group identity and cohesion ◇ Increasing intimacy and discussion of feelings ◇ Confronting the real issues ◇ Improved listening and feedback ◇ Moderate work accomplishment	
Performing	◇ High energy and productivity ◇ Flexible, open, close and supportive behaviours ◇ Settled interdependence ◇ High quality and creativity ◇ Maximum work accomplishment ◇ People enjoy the process	

Here's some of our answers.

Stage	Appropriate facilitator style
Forming	↳ Provide formal leadership to give structure. ↳ Use a highly directive approach. ↳ Make expectations clear – what, how, when and so on. ↳ Help group members become oriented towards task. ↳ Create an atmosphere of confidence. ↳ Establish temporary subgroups to enhance interactions. ↳ Use structured 'getting-acquainted' activities. ↳ Gradually introduce more relationship-building behaviours, as you judge the group is ready. ↳ Clarify goals, check expectations and establish norms. ↳ Contract with group members.
Storming	↳ Continue providing task direction, but now add relationship behaviours. ↳ Manage conflict – too much leads to chaos; too little leads to apathy. ↳ Help group members assume more responsibility. ↳ Support, praise and encourage – model active listening, and encourage others to listen. ↳ Confront unhelpful behaviours. ↳ Input training on skills, techniques and so on. ↳ Assign roles and functions. ↳ Watch for particularly 'stinging' feedback at this stage – emphasize ground rules and remind group of contract.
Norming	↳ Reduce amount of direction and structure given. ↳ Provide support. ↳ Encourage group to take over responsibility. ↳ Foster celebration – develop mottoes, symbols, logos and take group photos to help foster group identity. ↳ Encourage sharing, helping, listening, questioning and building. ↳ Try to avoid group membership changes at this stage.
Performing	↳ Turn over responsibility entirely to group – if you have done your job well, you are now not needed! ↳ Periodically reinforce achievement where appropriate. ↳ Gear any interventions towards maintaining this phase.

20 Brain-friendly beliefs about learning

Your beliefs set a ceiling on what you can accomplish. Simply having empowering beliefs alone does not guarantee success in an area, but they *are* a necessary precondition. Beliefs act like an inner 'thermostat' determining what is and what is not possible (whether you believe you can, or you believe you can't, you're probably right).

Beliefs are not fixed and unchangeable, although traditional therapies often assume they are. Prove this to yourself by thinking back to something you used to believe, but no longer do. (In fact, you might even be a tiny bit embarrassed that you used to believe it!)

Changing a belief will have more impact, like a ripple effect, on your behaviour, and therefore your results, than changing a behaviour will have on your belief system.

Beliefs tend to come in 'swarms' or 'clusters' – like buses, they seldom come alone! When working with changing beliefs, it is very common to sort one belief out only to find that another one pops up that has hitherto been beyond conscious awareness. This phenomenon, although it can be frustrating, is highly productive. Think of it like peeling the layers off an onion. Get curious!

Types of beliefs

GLOBAL BELIEFS

- ○ I am . . .
- ○ People are . . .
- ○ Life is . . .
- ○ Learning is . . .
- ○ I can't . . .
- ○ People should . . .
- ○ People shouldn't . . .
- ○ The world is . . .
- ○ Men are . . .
- ○ Women are . . .
- ○ Engineers are . . .
- ○ Old people are . . .
- ○ Teenagers are . . .
- ○ Organizations are . . .
- ○ Change is . . .
- ○ The future is . . .

IF . . . THEN RULES

○ If you trust people, they take advantage of you.
○ If I even look at a biscuit, I put on weight.
○ If you want to make it in this company, then you have to be tough.
○ If I can't get my own way, I must get angry.
○ If you loved me, you'd understand what I need without me having to tell you.

Activity: Beliefs and feelings

Beliefs can be empowering or limiting, depending on the circumstances. Look at the examples below, and think about how you would feel if you genuinely held this belief to be true. Then make up a couple of examples of your own.

Limiting beliefs	If you believed this, how would you feel?	Empowering belief	If you believed this, how would you feel?
Life's a bitch and then you die.		Life's a bowl of cherries.	
People are out to get you. Be careful!		People go out of their way to help me. Isn't it great?	
Change is slow, painful and never really works long-term.		Change is a natural, inevitable process, which can be enjoyed and learned from.	
Life is tough.		Life is what you make it.	
Add your own examples . . .		*Add your own examples . . .*	

21 Trapping your beliefs

'Nothing is good or bad, but thinking makes it so.' (William Shakespeare)

Events have no meaning other than the meaning you give them. A large part of how we all make meaning is based on our beliefs. Think of beliefs as a bit like an operating system in a computer – they are the general rules that are applied in different situations.

It can sometimes be challenging to work out your underlying beliefs – they are not always apparent, even to the person who holds them. Here's an activity that will give you practice in doing this.

Activity: Trap your beliefs . . .

Think of three 'bad' or negative experiences (events, states, crises) from your training experience and list them in the left-hand column. Make some notes about what the experience 'meant' and the feelings you had. Then complete the underlying belief in the right-hand column. What must you have believed in order to formulate that meaning or experience that feeling?

Experience	Meaning/Feeling	Belief

Now think of three 'good' or empowering experiences (events, states, peak moments) from your training experience and list them in the left-hand column. Again, jot down some notes about what this meant to you, and the associated feelings. Then complete the underlying belief in the right-hand column. What must you have believed in order to formulate that meaning or experience that feeling?

Experience	Meaning/Feeling	Belief

Beliefs about learning

Typically, trainers fall into one of three philosophical 'camps'.

Humanistic	Cognitive	Behaviourist
◇ Ask ◇ Elicit ◇ Intrinsic motivation ◇ Learner is resourceful ◇ 'Educare' – to draw out	◇ Tell ◇ Transmit ◇ Learner is 'empty vessel'	◇ Reinforce ◇ Strengthen ◇ Extrinsic motivation ◇ Learner must be 'controlled'

Where do you sit most comfortably? Brain-friendly learning sits firmly in column 1, the humanistic camp. The questionnaire below will give you an insight into your current beliefs – and challenge you to explore them further.

Activity: Beliefs questionnaire

Indicate how much you agree or disagree with the following statements about training and learning:

Statement	Strongly agree	Agree	Neither agree nor disagree	Disagree	Strongly disagree
Trainers should know a lot more than their learners about the topic – they should be the expert.					
A quiet room is generally needed for effective learning.					
Learners aren't ready for 'meaningful' discussion until they have acquired the basic facts.					
Learners should have the information given to them in bite-sized, linear chunks that build up to the whole picture.					
Some subjects are, by nature, boring or difficult, and there's nothing the trainer can do about this. People just have to get on with it.					
Learning is the consumption of information from an 'expert' source.					
Some delegates are just difficult – a good trainer needs to manage this.					
If a participant becomes confused by something, the trainer has not done their job properly.					
Some people just don't enjoy learning.					
Learners should all go through the same experience – that way, it's easier to evaluate the results.					

Now check whether your beliefs reflect brain-friendly learning principles.

Actually, we don't believe *any* of these statements. Here's why:

Statement	Our beliefs
Trainers should know a lot more than their learners about the topic – they should be the 'expert'.	Not necessarily. Trainers should be experts in the processes of human learning. Information is readily available – but really understanding how you can help somebody else learn elegantly and enjoyably is a rare skill. The main job of a facilitator is to create the right environment and the right state – learners can do the rest themselves.
A quiet room is generally needed for effective learning.	For some people, some of the time, this may be true. However, a rich and multisensory environment creates lots of stimulation that can aid learning. Certain kinds of background music have certainly been shown to aid learning and retention.
Learners aren't ready for 'meaningful' discussion until they have acquired the basic facts.	Humans are meaning-making creatures – in fact, they cannot not make meaning. Meaningful discussion aids learning at any point in the process.
Learners should have the information given to them in bite-sized, linear chunks that build up to the whole picture.	Many people prefer to have the big picture first. Also, our brains are parallel processors and are capable of creating meaning and new connections at many different levels simultaneously.
Some subjects are, by nature, boring or difficult, and there's nothing the trainer can do about this. People just have to get on with it.	The trainer, and the learners, can do a great deal to make any subject fascinating. As well as creating personally meaningful goals, we can get into a state of curiosity, excitement or resourcefulness – regardless of the topic.
Learning is the consumption of information from an 'expert' source.	Learning is the creation of value and meaning: there need not always be an 'expert' source. In fact, business in the twenty-first century needs more people who question, challenge and innovate, rather than simply accept the received wisdom.
Some delegates are just difficult – a good trainer needs to manage this.	There's no such thing as a difficult delegate – only an inflexible trainer. Honouring uniqueness means finding out what will work for that person.
If a participant becomes confused by something, the trainer has not done their job properly.	A certain amount of confusion aids learning. If your participants become confused, celebrate! It means they are just about to make a breakthrough!
Some people just don't enjoy learning.	Maybe some people just don't enjoy learning in the ways we are teaching? Find another way.
Learners should all go through the same experience – that way, it's easier to evaluate the results.	Evaluate results by looking at how the learning has been applied back in the organization. There's no reason why people should have the same experience. Again, honour uniqueness.

Activity: Exploring your beliefs about learning

1. Look for at least three articles in recent issues of a magazine or your local newspaper. These can be either explicitly or implicitly about learning.
2. Identify at least one belief in each article about learning, learners or training, noting that it may be stated openly or merely implied. You may or may not agree with this belief.
3. Summarize your thoughts about 'what society seems to believe about the nature of learning'. You can choose to do this in one of the following ways:
   - Write a brief article for a newsletter on brain-friendly learning.
   - Prepare to tell a story to a group of novice trainers.
   - Create a short sketch or role-play.
   - Draw a picture or Mind Map®.
   - Compare a song, limerick, poem or jingle.
   - Imagine you are about to have a conversation with the authors of the articles. What would you say? What would you ask?
4. Now reflect on your own beliefs. What have you learned about yourself as a facilitator of learning?
5. Share your findings and reflections with other trainers – compare your interpretations. What are the implicit beliefs about learning in your organization?

22 Generative learning

'Give a man a fish and you feed him for a day, teach him how to fish and you feed him for life.'

There is a story told in NLP circles about when Gregory Bateson – the great systems theorist and writer – went to study the communication patterns of dolphins at the Marine Research Institute in Hawaii, described in his book, *Steps to an Ecology of Mind*.[22]

Bateson observed as the trainers taught dolphins to perform at public shows. When a new trainee dolphin did something unusual, such as jumping out of the water in a certain way, the trainer blew a whistle and threw the dolphin a fish as a reward. Every time the dolphin demonstrated that particular behaviour, the trainer would repeat the whistle and the reward.

Very soon the dolphin learned that in order to get a fish, it should perform that particular jump. This is simple behavioural conditioning through reinforcement, and there's nothing astonishing about the fact that it works to train dolphins – we've known this since Pavlov and his salivating dogs.

The next day, the dolphin would be brought out into the pool again and do the jump, expecting a nice juicy fish. But no fish would be forthcoming. The dolphin would repeat its jump for some time, and then – out of frustration, probably – would do something different, such as rolling over. Immediately, the trainer would blow the whistle and throw it a fish. No fish for yesterday's trick, only for something new.

This pattern was repeated for two weeks. The dolphin would come out and do the trick it had learned yesterday – but only a new trick would elicit a fish. Sometimes, the dolphin would 'throw in' a few tricks from last week just to test the rules. However, it was only rewarded when it did something new.

On the fifteenth day, the dolphin suddenly went into generative learning – it came into the pool and gave a completely astonishing show, rolling, jumping and doing double back-flips. According to the trainers watching, the dolphin did eight completely new tricks that day, including four that had never been observed in the species before! The dolphin had finally learned the rules.

One final interesting point from this story is to do with rapport. Bateson noticed that sometimes the trainer threw the dolphin unearned fish outside the training sessions. When he asked the trainer about this, he replied 'Well, trainers need a superb relationship with the dolphin – otherwise why should they bother at all?'

As a facilitator, if you can help people learn how to learn even better, you are providing the most valuable service one human being can provide to another.

There's a lot of talk about the 'learning organization' these days – quite rightly. Generative learning is the key. This is the difference between giving somebody a fish, and teaching them how to fish. People who have learned how to learn have a much wider repertoire of choices, and they don't need to be spoonfed.

Activity: Generative learning

Consider the programme for a learning event you are designing or facilitating. Identify at least five ways you could increase the potential for your participants to experience generative learning, whilst still meeting the agreed learning outcomes:

1.

2.

3.

4.

5.

Now take a session where you hitherto would have 'structured' the learning method for the learners. Brief them in the normal way, making sure that you clarify the outcomes, and then invite them to generate new ways of learning for themselves. In other words, don't provide them with a structured activity.

When debriefing the activity, ask them to close the learning cycle loop with high-quality questions such as

○ 'Where else could you use this?'
○ 'What have you learned about learning?'
○ 'What observations and generalizations would you make now about your own learning choices?'

'The only sustainable competitive advantage is the ability to learn faster than your competitors.' (Arie de Geus)

Tools for honouring uniqueness

23 Two modes of processing

You've just started a new job in a large factory. At lunchtime your stomach is rumbling but you don't know where to find the staff canteen. A colleague gives you directions: 'Take the lift to the third floor, turn right and then left at the end of the corridor.' You follow her instructions and, sure enough, they lead you to the canteen. This is **explicit** learning. Someone tells you what you need to know in a clear, rational way and you process that information consciously and logically.

After lunch, instead of retracing your steps, you decide to wander about for a bit. After a while, you come back to a bit of the plant you recognize, and return to your office. You do this each day after lunch for a week or so, until you begin to feel confident that you know your way around. This is **implicit** learning. It's a little messy, somewhat experiential, and it works at an unconscious level. It's not as if you studied a map of the plant and consciously set out to explore each nook and cranny – that would be an explicit approach too. Instead, you just wander around and learn the geography, by osmosis as it were.

Here are some words and phrases that capture the essence of each style of learning.

Explicit		Implicit	
Logical	Declarative	Intuitive	Procedural
Rational	Requires effort	Holistic	Automatic
Left brain	Facts	Right brain	Feelings
Conscious	Didactic	Unconscious	Experiential
Semantic	Mechanistic	Episodic	Organic

We can all learn in both modes, but most people have a preference for one mode or the other. If you take care to address both modes on a learning event, this will ensure that everyone is able to learn not only with their preferred mode, but also with a complementary one.

Activity: Two modes of processing

Write down in the space below a short outline of the sessions in a training course for which you are responsible. Against each session write in whether it is mainly explicit learning, mainly implicit learning or a mixture of both. In the light of this insight, what changes do you need to make in the course design?

24 Different angles – 4-MAT

A very useful addition to the 4-MAT approach to designing learning has been provided by Bernice McCarthy.[5] Although this concept comes mainly from the world of formal education, the principles can be applied successfully to business settings.

In this approach, the teacher's role changes as they move through the cycle of learning:

- ❍ from Motivator/Witness
- ❍ to Teacher/Information Giver
- ❍ to Facilitator/Coach
- ❍ to Evaluator and Resource.

The figure below shows how the Teacher's role changes as students move through the four stages of learning.

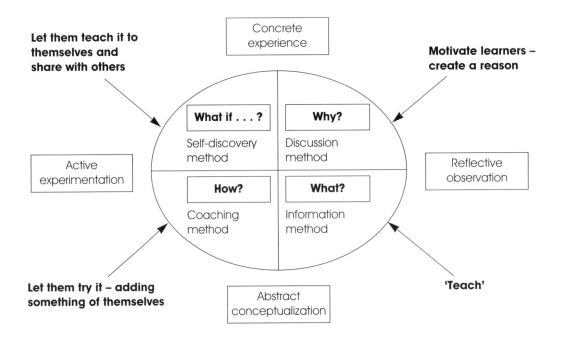

4-MAT preferences

Once again, note that individual students will have preferences in terms of the fundamental question they **must** answer for themselves in order to 'learn' successfully. For some people, the sequence is important too – they must know 'why?' before they can make sense of 'how?', for example. A good check is to ensure that your design allows an opportunity for them to 'answer' all four questions.

Activity: Balancing your 4-MAT

Take a course you are currently involved in, and analyse whether there are opportunities for the learners to 'answer' all four key questions about your material and calculate the relative proportion of time spent on each key question. Fill these in below:

Why?   %
What?   %
How?   %
What if . . . ?   %

The appropriate proportions will be influenced, to some extent, by the specific learning outcomes. However, regardless of the emphasis, your design should allow at least some time on each of the four.

How well balanced are your proportions? What could you do to improve this?

25 Multiple intelligences

Here's a short description of each of the ten intelligences, and some examples of how they can be inspired and engaged during learning events:

Interpersonal

Characteristics: an aptitude for understanding, empathizing and communicating with other people; the ability to step into other people's shoes and see the world from their point of view. Our relationships with others are managed through this intelligence.

Under stress: talks to somebody about the problem.

Creative strategy: bounces ideas off others.

Appropriate training methods:

- ○ work in pairs, threes or teams – keep mixing up the groups
- ○ contracting – groundrules that emphasize collaboration and trust
- ○ change leadership roles
- ○ giving and receiving feedback
- ○ team competition or quiz
- ○ learners train each other
- ○ articulating learning to each other
- ○ role-plays
- ○ question and answer session, debate, discussion
- ○ coaching or study buddy.

Logical/mathematical

Characteristics: an aptitude for processing analytically; being good at calculating, quantifying and carrying out steps in a sequence. Tends to be highly valued in business.

Under stress: adds up the pros and cons of the problem analytically.

Creative strategy: breaks down the problem into concrete, do-able steps.

Appropriate training methods:

- ○ pre-exposure with big picture
- ○ using symbols/formulae
- ○ storyboarding

○ checklists
○ process maps
○ force field analysis
○ cause and effect diagrams
○ flowcharts
○ assigning numbers to things.

Visual/spatial

Characteristics: an aptitude for thinking three-dimensionally, seeing, imagining and creating pictures – both inside the mind and externally.

Under stress: escapes through movies (real or imagined).

Creative strategy: creates visual representations of positive or negative outcomes – sees things happening. Paints or draws.

Appropriate training methods:

○ Mind Maps®, thematics or spider diagrams
○ posters and pictures
○ peripherals
○ film and video
○ pictograms
○ guided visualization or imagery, mental rehearsal
○ use of colour and colour coding
○ meta-planning
○ spatial anchors
○ larger than life gestures by the facilitator
○ visually interesting handouts and materials
○ highly visual visual aids!

Musical/rhythmic

Characteristics: a sensitivity to pitch, rhythm, tone and melody; an enjoyment of music – either as a composer, performer or listener. According to Gardner's research[1] it is the earliest form of human giftedness to emerge in child prodigies.

Under stress: listens to music.

Creative strategy: listens to music or plays an instrument in order to think more creatively.

Appropriate training methods:

- ○ rhythmic tonal patterns in speech
- ○ exaggerate volume, tone and intonation
- ○ music
- ○ humming
- ○ singing and writing songs
- ○ writing and peforming rap or poetry
- ○ emphasizing key points with sound – for example, clapping, banging the table or whistling.

Linguistic/verbal

Characteristics: an aptitude for expressing thoughts clearly through the spoken or written word. Highly valued in business.

Under stress: captures thoughts in a journal, escapes into a book.

Creative strategy: uses metaphors and stories to generate new ideas. Reading what others have said or thought inspires their own creativity.

Appropriate training methods:

- ○ reading – books or handouts
- ○ speaking and presenting
- ○ journal or learning log/diary
- ○ creative writing
- ○ debate
- ○ storytelling
- ○ use descriptive, inspiring words
- ○ verbal humour
- ○ composing poems or raps
- ○ word-search or crosswords linked to the theme of the training.

Intrapersonal

Characteristics: an aptitude for accessing wisdom through reflection; good at thinking things through, processing events and experiences and then reaching some new learning as a result of this. Most organizations suffer because people have less and less time for this important activity – often the whole day is taken up with meetings. People often need more time just to sit and think. Don't just do something, sit there!

Under stress: withdraw to find a space where they can be alone, go for long walks, shuns all company.

Creative strategy: sits and thinks.

Appropriate training methods:

- ○ active or passive concert reviews
- ○ time for private reflection – perhaps with some key questions
- ○ time for individual thoughts before and after group activities
- ○ meditation
- ○ complex guided imagery
- ○ spiral learning – introduce topic lightly, drop it, come back later, activate, layer it
- ○ embedding using unconscious mind
- ○ learning journal or diary.

Bodily/kinaesthetic

Characteristics: an aptitude for physical movement and using the body.

Under stress: works out, goes for a long run, undertakes some hard physical labour.

Creative strategy: thinks whilst throwing a ball around, or clicking a pen, or just pacing.

Appropriate training methods:

- ○ movement – change seating frequently
- ○ role-play, drama or mime
- ○ physically active games and activities – for example, scavenger hunts
- ○ laminated cards with key points (highly tactile)
- ○ presenter gestures and body language
- ○ regular breaks
- ○ artefacts and manipulatives – things to touch/feel in the environment (people who need to learn by keeping active can be highly fidgety – provide things for them to play with)
- ○ use of physical or sporting metaphors
- ○ 3D model-making – sculpture or collage
- ○ brain gym and energizers
- ○ encouragement to stand up and walk around if this helps them learn better.

And the more recent three intelligences – **N**ever **E**at **E**lephants!

Naturalist

Characteristics: an aptitude for appreciating and being with nature. People with a well-developed naturalist intelligence are typically very concerned about the environment and about ecology. Part of this aptitude is the ability to categorize – to survive in nature, it is essential to be able to distinguish between something edible and something poisonous or a creature that will befriend you versus one that will eat you!

Under stress: goes outside, gardens, hikes, walks, climbs mountains.

Creative strategy: goes outside and gains strength and inspiration from nature.

Appropriate training methods:

- plenty of natural light in the learning environment
- nature scenes on the walls
- outside activities
- 'nature breaks'
- outdoor 'walkie-talkie' exercises
- fresh flowers and plants in the learning environment
- sorting and categorizing activities
- 'ecology' checks ('What are the environmental implications of this?', 'How could this preserve the planet or the species?').

Emotional

Characteristics: an aptitude for recognizing emotions and reacting to them in ways considered positive by the culture. Popularized by Daniel Goleman in his bestselling book, *Emotional Intelligence*.[6] Notice the similarity between this intelligence and the intrapersonal and bodily/feeling intelligences. Remember, too, that learning attached to emotions will be the easiest to embed into long-term memory, as it is processed through the limbic brain.

Under stress: withdraws into self to identify true feelings.

Creative strategy: does an emotional check – weighs each idea against how it 'feels'.

Appropriate training methods:

- processing of learning through emotions: 'How did that feel?'
- music to calm or excite emotions
- individual reflection
- morning check-ins and end-of-day check-outs that allow people to express their feelings about the way the learning is going for them
- spatial line-ups or 'emotional thermometers' that capture how participants' feelings change throughout the experience.

Existential

Characteristics: an aptitude for knowing the purpose of existence – having a sense of personal mission.

Under stress: remembers their personal mission.

Creative strategy: aligns creative pursuits to personal goals.

Appropriate training methods:

- ❍ 'future pacing' activities – guided imagery that links the learning to successful goal accomplishment back at work
- ❍ encouraging participants to create clear and compelling learning goals that have real meaning for their lives
- ❍ creating personal mission statements and anchoring the learning to these
- ❍ reinforcement of shared values and visions.

26 Inspiring and engaging all the intelligences

Here are some ideas that help activate the different intelligences.

LINGUISTIC/VERBAL	**MUSICAL/RHYTHMIC**
◇ Reading – books or handouts ◇ Speeches and presentations ◇ Journal or learning diary ◇ Creative writing (i.e. a film script) ◇ Debate ◇ Storytelling	◇ Rhythmic patterns (music, speech) ◇ Vocal sounds and tone ◇ Music ◇ Humming ◇ Singing/song writing ◇ Performing with music ◇ Writing and performing rap or poetry
BODILY/KINAESTHETIC	**LOGICAL/MATHEMATICAL**
◇ Brain gym ◇ Movement and dance ◇ Role-play, drama and mime ◇ Games ◇ Presenter gestures/body language ◇ Regular breaks ◇ Artifacts and manipulatives ◇ 3D model-making ◇ Sculpture or collage	◇ Pre-exposure with big picture ◇ Using symbols/formulae ◇ Outlining ◇ Numbers and calculation ◇ Problem-solving ◇ Pattern review ◇ Flowcharts ◇ Process mapping ◇ Storyboarding
INTERPERSONAL	**VISUAL/SPATIAL**
◇ Giving feedback ◇ Collaborative exercises ◇ Discussion or question and answer ◇ Group or team projects ◇ Coaching others ◇ Training others ◇ Getting feedback ◇ Working with how people feel ◇ Team competition or quiz ◇ Present to peers ◇ Expert/reporter interviews	◇ Pre-exposure with big picture, Mind Maps® and patterns ◇ Visualization and mental rehearsal ◇ Imagination ◇ Colour codes ◇ Patterns and designs ◇ Painting and drawing ◇ Mind Maps® ◇ Meta-planning ◇ Posters and peripherals ◇ Thematics and spider diagrams
INTRAPERSONAL	**NATURALIST**
◇ Meditation ◇ Thinking ◇ Emotional content – processed internally ◇ High-order reasoning ◇ Complex guided imagery ◇ Spiral learning – introduce topic lightly, drop it, come back later, activate, layer it ◇ Embedding using unconscious mind ◇ Time to reflect quietly – perhaps with some key questions	◇ 'Ecological checks' on the subject you are exploring, asking key questions such as: What are the environmental implications of what you are learning? Will it help or hinder social fairness? Can it help us solve social problems? Does it guide you to any action that will preserve or prolong species? (Note: offers less value in many subjects, but still often worth exploring.)

Activity: Designing an induction programme

Now that you are familiar with the idea of multiple intelligences, it is time to put them to work in the training and learning context.

Design a one-day induction programme to give new employees an overview of your company. Sketch out a session plan for the event, which includes at least eight activities. Each activity should appeal primarily to one of the eight intelligences. Don't worry if some of your ideas seem a bit way-out at this stage – just have fun!

Session	Activities	Intelligence
1		
2		
3		
4		
5		
6		
7		
8		

Of course, there is no single right answer to this activity. Here's one way of tackling it. How does this approach compare with yours?

Session	Activities	Intelligence
1	Overview, icebreakers and personal introductions	Interpersonal
2	Participants are taken on a tour around the factory	Bodily/kinaesthetic
3	Participants work in small groups to produce a collage about the company, using material cut from annual reports and the company's in-house newsletter	Visual/spatial
4	The managing director gives a short talk about the company and invites questions and debate	Linguistic/verbal
5	Relaxing music is played in the background while the participants are given a list of questions to reflect on individually. The questions help them to clarify what they can contribute to the company and what other information they need at this stage	Intrapersonal
6	The finance director gives participants a simplified version of the company accounts and asks them to tell her where the company is doing well and where it could do better	Logical/mathematical
7	A group of existing staff makes a presentation about the history of the company, using the metaphor of a small seed that has grown into a tree with many branches	Naturalist
8	In groups, the participants compose and deliver a song, limerick or a nursery rhyme that summarizes what they have learnt today about the company	

27 Developing your own intelligences

In this section we've tended to suggest that any given training activity tends to appeal primarily to just one intelligence. However, many training activities appeal to more than one – a good role-play exercise, for example, will appeal to interpersonal, intrapersonal, bodily feeling and linguistic intelligences, at least. So, as you continue with this manual, honing and developing your skills as a people learner, be alert for opportunities to devise training activities that appeal to as many intelligences as possible.

One way to develop this kind of sensitivity is to work systematically on your own intelligences. You will find useful ideas in the following resource box.

Building your intelligences

LINGUISTIC/VERBAL	MUSICAL/RHYTHMIC
◇ Play word games – for example, Scrabble, crosswords, anagrams. ◇ Keep a daily diary. ◇ Find opportunities to tell stories. ◇ Make up your own riddles, puns and jokes. ◇ Join a book club, and/or attend a creative writing workshop. ◇ Teach somebody to read and write.	◇ Join a choir, or just sing in your car, in the shower – anywhere! ◇ Learn to play a musical instrument. ◇ Listen for naturally occurring rhythms in footsteps, birdsong – even washing machines! ◇ Make up a jingle, rap or rhyme of things you want to remember. ◇ Listen to background music whilst doing other things.
BODILY/KINAESTHETIC	**LOGICAL/MATHEMATICAL**
◇ Learn juggling, yoga, the Japanese tea ceremony, dancing, massage. ◇ Learn sign language or Braille. ◇ Take up a sport. ◇ Do hobbies and crafts such as woodworking, sewing, pottery or weaving, gardening, cooking, model-building. ◇ Just put some music on and move!	◇ Play logical games – for example, Go, Cluedo, logic puzzles. ◇ Draw flowcharts of key processes in your business. ◇ Visit a science museum. ◇ Learn basic computer programming.
INTERPERSONAL	**VISUAL/SPATIAL**
◇ Join a volunteer group, such as the Samaritans. ◇ Spend at least 30 minutes each day listening actively to the people around you. ◇ Throw parties and invite people you don't know very well. ◇ Make a list of all the people you love – and tell them all this week. ◇ Model great communicators – find out what works for them.	◇ Use Mind Maps®. ◇ Incorporate more pictures, photos and diagrams into your written work. ◇ Visit art galleries. ◇ Design a garden, a house, or a colour scheme. ◇ Play Pictionary and other visual games. ◇ Take a class in painting, graphic design, sculpting or photography.
INTRAPERSONAL	**NATURALIST**
◇ Learn to meditate. ◇ Keep a diary, or even write your autobiography. ◇ Study philosophy, especially from different cultures. ◇ Establish a quiet place for introspection, and create your own rituals. ◇ write down your dreams – and make a life plan.	◇ Spend time outdoors. ◇ Visit the Natural History Museum. ◇ Create collections of natural things . ◇ Study an ant colony, or bees collecting pollen. ◇ Change your surroundings depending on the season.

28 Meta-programmes

Big picture/small detail

Larry once worked with a trainer called Naomi and, together, they had a great deal of trouble designing courses. The conversation would go something like this.

> **Larry**: Let's start with thinking about our overall objectives for this course.

> **Naomi**: We can worry about that later – what we need to know now is what time do we start and finish the course, and when are the coffee breaks?

Larry was horrified that Naomi considered such mundane things as break times were more important than the overall course objectives. Naomi thought that Larry had his head in the clouds with abstract philosophical concepts when they hadn't even agreed the most basic practicalities of how long they'd have to deliver the course!

What was going on here? Naomi and Larry had different ways of processing information. He was much more interested in the big picture – what was this course all about? What did we want participants to learn? Naomi was much more interested in the small details – what were the start and finishing times? How many chairs would we need in the training room?

Most people tend to be more comfortable either with the big picture or with the small details. But, of course, you need both. As a big picture person, Larry tended to overlook the small details. For example, his course handouts would contain numerous spelling mistakes and he'd forget to make sure that the refreshments would arrive on time. As a small detail person, Naomi ran the risk of confusing participants by leaping straight into the technical details of a topic without putting it properly into context first. In fact, once Naomi and Larry realized what was going on, and that their perspectives complemented each other, they made a great training team.

In any group of participants, you will tend to get a mixture of big picture people and small detail people. How do you make sure that both groups have a good learning experience? The solution is to present learning opportunities which meet the needs of both groups. Let's say you are leading an event on performance appraisal. Make sure you cover the big picture – why do we need an appraisal system? What are the major elements of an appraisal system? And also make sure you cover the small details – how exactly does it work? What are the company's specific procedures for appraisal?

Certain professions tend to attract people with certain ways of thinking. Would you expect the following professions to attract big picture or small detail people?

- Entrepreneurs
- Accountants
- Lawyers
- Marketing professionals.

Our answers would be big picture for entrepreneurs, small detail for accountants and lawyers and – less obviously – probably big picture for marketing. So if you were facilitating a learning event for, say, a group of accountants you might want to ensure that they are given plenty of small detail to get their teeth into.

Beware of stereotyping people, though. Although most people have a preference one way or the other, we can all deal with big picture and small detail to some extent. And a few people are equally at home with either.

This distinction – small detail or big picture – is often described as a meta-programme and is one of a number. Here are some other meta-programmes which are particularly relevant to facilitators of learning.

Match/mismatch

Some people tend to look for points of similarity – we call them matchers. Some tend to look for points of difference – we call them mismatchers. During a training event on leadership, a discussion between two participants goes like this:

> **Andrea**: Our chief executive is a bit like Churchill – he's brilliant at making tremendously inspiring speeches, but he's sometimes a bit full of his own self-importance.

> **Bill**: I'm not sure that's a very good analogy – leading a business is very different to leading a country.

From this snippet you could tentatively judge Andrea as a matcher and Bill as the mismatcher.

Towards/away from

Some people are much more interested in moving towards a better future, while others focus more on getting away from the past. Imagine a consultancy firm which had two very good, but contrasting, consultants. Gary was very much an 'away from' person. He'd begin a new consultancy assignment by spending a lot of time asking the client to detail everything that was wrong with the company, so that he could come up with a plan for moving the company on. Keith, by contrast, used the opposite approach. He never asked anything about the history of the company – his focus was on how the company wanted to be in the future.

Understanding this meta-programme is especially important if you facilitate learning events around the topic of change. Typically, change leaders tend to have more of 'towards' orientation. They repeatedly emphasize the vision, and how wonderful the company will be in the future. Many of the people who have to listen to this may have more of an 'away from' orientation. They won't be interested in all this 'vision' – what they want to know is how the changes will help them get away from some of the things that they currently don't like in the company.

Activity: Musing on meta-programmes

Think about a recent learning event you facilitated, and identify two people on that event who you felt hadn't got as much value out of it as you would have wished. Complete the following table for you and for those two people:

Person	Big picture/ small detail	Match/ mismatch	Towards/ away from
You			
Person A:			
Person B:			

Now analyse this data. If you were running this event for these people again, how would you structure it differently?

Tools for making it rich and multisensory

29 An environment that says 'you matter'

The learning environment

Activity: Best and worst

Imagine you wanted to create the very *worst* possible training environment. Brainstorm a list of everything you could do to create a training room that was sure to put people in a very unresourceful state. You may want to draw on some real-life experiences!

Now turn the list around – based on your brainstorm, create a checklist for an ideal training venue.

Now compare your list with ours on page 150.

THE PHYSICAL ENVIRONMENT: WHY IT MATTERS

Our state is dependent on two main factors – our physiology and our mental focus. The physical environment of the training event can have a big impact on both of these. If a training room is too hot or too cold, stuffy, cramped or physically uncomfortable, it will have a direct and detrimental effect on the physiology of the participants. If the training room is tacky and tatty, or looks more like a prison cell or the interview room at a police station, then this will have a direct and detrimental effect on the mental state of the participants.

At a minimum, you can remove some of these negative effects of the training room. Better still, you can take active steps to create a learning environment which in itself helps participants to get into a positive state.

'Dressing the room' has another important pay-off too – a rich and colourful environment has been shown to actually stimulate dendritic branching in the brain. Put simply, your learners will become smarter. Research has also shown that the information in carefully placed peripherals (for example, posters) is taken in by learners at the unconscious level.

KEY INFLUENCES IN THE ENVIRONMENT

Listed below are some of the factors that you, as a facilitator, can influence in the training environment.

Multisensory atmosphere

- ○ Negative ionization
- ○ Temperature
- ○ Lighting
- ○ Colours
- ○ Noise levels
- ○ Aromas
- ○ Music.

Peripherals

- ○ Posters
- ○ Visual aids
- ○ Artifacts
- ○ Manipulatives (things they can touch)
- ○ (Relevant) toys and table top themes
- ○ Mobiles
- ○ Wall, floor and ceiling displays.

Nature

- ○ Plants and flowers
- ○ Natural light.

Materials

- ○ Handouts
- ○ Manuals
- ○ Workbooks
- ○ Resource table.

Room arrangements and seating options

Arrange the furniture so that learners can see each other, as well as you. Make it easy for people to move around and change groups quickly.

A positive social environment

Build in a successful experience in the first 20 minutes. Include a collaborative pre-test, icebreaker or other connecting activities.

A positive emotional environment

Consider positive suggestions, learner benefits, sharing goals, allaying concerns and evoking good feelings, and anchor these to the material.

Training venue basic checklist

- ○ Clear signage so that people can find the venue.
- ○ Notice by door with name of training course.
- ○ Comfortable room temperature – able to be varied.
- ○ Adequate ventilation.

○ Adequate lighting – preferably natural light. Fluorescents raise cortisol levels and are thought by some to lower the immune system.

○ Soundproofing.

○ Some natural daylight.

○ Comfortable chairs.

○ Water to drink.

○ Easily available refreshments.

○ Toilets nearby.

○ Enough space for the number of participants – as a rule of thumb, at least 4 sq m per person.

○ Appropriate audiovisual equipment – flipcharts, data projector, OHP, video player and TV, computers.

○ Minimum clutter (move old computer equipment, unwanted furniture and any other junk out of your training environment).

○ A learner-friendly room arrangement (where learners can see each other).

○ Movement, contrast and colour changes. Use more visuals, more motion in the visuals, and more changes in location. Make use of visually exciting videos, vivid drawings, symbols, posters and murals. Bring things in to show and tell. Ask the learners to visualize.

○ Peripherals. These are picked up by the unconscious mind (especially when colour coded), and actually gain in impact over time. Research shows that peripherals create effortless, subject-specific, longer-lasting recall. (See Tool 30, 'Dressing the learning environment'.)

30 Dressing the learning environment

Enhancing the venue with peripherals

A barren training room suggests a barren learning experience. Peripherals – that is, objects and displays that add interest and colour can create a learning environment that is positive, stimulating, supportive, relaxing and creative. When used well, peripherals create positive states in the learner, provide constant reinforcement and enhance the learning process.

Surrounding the learner with stimuli

Peripherals surround the learner with materials from a course. Training rooms can become multisensory walk-in textbooks. In the same way that we all learned how to speak our native tongue because we were constantly exposed to it in our homes, we can help our learners to learn in context. Peripherals can take a wide variety of forms, and a few ideas are suggested below.

WALL DISPLAYS

❍ Posters
❍ Pictures
❍ Banners
❍ Velcro boards
❍ Art prints
❍ Signs
❍ System flowcharts
❍ Computer screens

CEILING DISPLAYS

❍ Mobiles
❍ Stars, clouds, planets
❍ Kites

TABLE TOP DISPLAYS

❍ Equipment
❍ Mock-ups

○ Miniature environments
○ Manipulable objects
○ Flowers or plants

OBJECTS

○ Toys
○ Athletic equipment
○ Household items
○ Cardboard blocks
○ Pillows or beanbags

UPRIGHT ITEMS

○ Flipcharts
○ Sign posts
○ Pinboards
○ Free-standing displays
○ Floor plants

FLOOR DISPLAYS

○ 'Steps' in a business process
○ Path through a system
○ Large blueprints
○ Coloured shapes

DOOR DISPLAYS

○ Welcome poster
(Most people like to hear and read their own name. Help create a positive feeling at the outset of the course by displaying a flipchart saying 'Welcome' and listing the names of all the participants.)
○ Motivational or inspiring quotes
○ Thematic displays

DRESSING UP

○ Special clothing or hats
○ Costumes
○ Sandwich board

AUDIOVISUAL

❍ Music
❍ Music videos
❍ Computer screen with large, relevant screensaver or wallpaper

THEMES

In cases where you decide to use a theme, the peripherals will easily suggest themselves. A beach or cruise theme, for example, might call for nautical music, travel posters, large islands on the wall representing the major topics – with a cardboard cruise ship that moves from island to island as the course progresses. A Wizard of Oz theme might suggest a yellow brick road for the course map. A detective theme might use *Pink Panther* music, a rogues' gallery and large footprints on the floor as peripherals.

FRESH FLOWERS

Fresh flowers are highly recommended for any training event. As well as brightening up the training venue in a way that will offend no one, you can make someone's day when the course is over by giving them to a work colleague or friend as a present! However, we must sound a slight note of caution: any hayfever sufferers in the group might not appreciate these particular peripherals! Check with the group on the first morning – and use low-pollen flowers.

POSTERS

Posters constitute a quick and easy way to turn a dull room into a more inviting space for learning. Most of the good facilitators we know have their own set of laminated posters with 'inspirational' quotations which they bring with them to most courses. See the activity on page 155 on producing your own set of inspirational posters.

You can also use content-related posters. Many facilitators post flipcharts on to a wall during the course of a training event. Why not put up some ready-prepared flipcharts before the event? As well as making the room look good and helping to put people into a receptive state, it also exposes participants in advance to some of the material.

Depending on the subject matter of the course, you can also use appropriate professionally produced posters. When we run workshops on brain-friendly learning, for example, we display big posters explaining how the brain works.

NEGATIVELY CHARGED AIR

Have you ever stood near a really big waterfall? Do you remember the quality of the air?

Negatively charged air has been shown to speed recovery, affect seratonin levels in the bloodstream, stabilize alpha rhythms and positively influence reactions to sensory stimuli. Using an ionizer to increase the number of negative ions in the atmosphere not only creates a fresh feel to the air, it also helps boost alertness and learning in up to 85 per cent of learners. Make sure it's big enough for the room.

AROMAS

In evolutionary terms, smell is one of the oldest of the senses. The olfactory regions are rich receptor sites for endorphins, signalling the body's response to feelings of pleasure and well-being. Certain smells can have a tremendous impact on our state. The easiest way to produce appropriate smells is to use a burner with essential oils, obtainable from most wholefood shops. Alternatively, you can buy specially prepared sprays, designed to evoke different states (see 'Further resources' on page 226).

For energizing, try basil, peppermint, rosemary or cinnamon; for calming and relaxation, try lavender, chamomile, orange or rose.

MUSIC

This is such an important factor in creating a resourceful state that it deserves a whole section to itself – see Tool 44, 'Music' on page 203.

TIPS

Peripherals need not be elaborate or expensive, just aesthetically pleasing and educationally appropriate.

❍ Use bright colours in most cases.
❍ Make wall displays larger than life.
❍ Make large lettering.
❍ Change peripherals when new topics are introduced.
❍ Avoid clutter.
❍ Have learners make peripherals and add them to the existing ones.

Activity: Inspirational posters

A good way to transform a dull room into a more enticing one is to put up a number of colourful, motivational posters.

Make a list of your favourite motivational quotations. The quickest way to find these is to put 'quotations' into your Internet web browser and then look at some of the many Internet sites devoted to inspirational quotations. Be sure to check any copyright issues. Alternatively, feel free to use some or all of our favourite inspirational quotations set out in the list below.

Choose suitable graphics for each quotation.

Print in colour at least A3 size.

Laminate them so they stay looking good.

SOME OF OUR FAVOURITE INSPIRATIONAL QUOTATIONS

'Whether you believe you can, or you believe you can't – you're always right' (Henry Ford)

'Leadership is the capacity to create a compelling vision and translate it into action and sustain it.' (Warren Bennis)

'Whether you think that you can, or that you can't, you are usually right.' (Henry Ford)

'Do, or do not. There is no "try".' (Yoda, in *The Empire Strikes Back*)

'Never doubt that a small group of thoughtful, committed citizens can change the world. Indeed, it is the only thing that ever has.' (Margaret Mead)

'There is nothing good or bad, but thinking makes it so.' (William Shakespeare)

'We are disturbed not by things, but by the views we take of things.' (Epictetus)

'Imagination is more important than knowledge.' (Albert Einstein)

'It is not because things are difficult that we do not dare; it is because we do not dare they are difficult.' (Seneca)

'We learn to do something by doing it. There is no other way.' (John Holt)

'Whatever you can do, or dream you can, begin it.
Boldness has genius, power and magic in it.
Begin it now!' (Johann Wolfgang von Goethe)

Activity: Course makeover

Identify a forthcoming training course for which you are responsible.

Now, in the space below, list the actions you need to take to ensure that the basic training room is adequate.

List below the peripherals you need to enhance the training room.

31 Multichannel VHF

We learn through our senses, and especially through our senses of seeing, hearing and feeling. If you deliver training that appeals to all the senses, it will be much more powerful and effective than training that appeals to just one or two. This tool shows you how.

VHF in behaviour

We take in information about the world through our five senses. In particular we use our visual sense, hearing and feeling. In this manual we will refer to our:

- ○ visual sense – (V)
- ○ hearing – (H)
- ○ feeling – (F)

Hence the title of this chapter, 'Multichannel VHF'. When we refer to our sense of feeling, we'll include both physical feelings (such as picking up a hot cup) and emotional feelings (such as elation or anxiety).

Although most people use their visual, hearing and feeling senses to take in information about the world, it's very rare for anyone to use all three representational systems to an equal extent. Most of us have preferences.

Consider the following situation. You have just started work in a new office building and you want to find your way to the meeting room. You ask three different people and they respond in three different ways. From these brief descriptions, which person do you think is primarily visual, which person hearing and which person feeling?

- ○ Andrea sketches you a map on a piece of scrap paper.
- ○ Bill tells you how to get there: 'Go along the main corridor, turn left up the stairs . . .'
- ○ Corinne takes you by the arm and leads you to the meeting room herself.

Of course, it is dangerous to stereotype a person on the basis of such a small amount of information. But, given the above responses, the chances are that Andrea is visual, Bill is hearing and Corinne is feeling. Now let's say you arrive at the meeting and Andrea's presentation involves lots of visual aids, Bill basically delivers a spoken lecture (perhaps livened up with a bit of music and some quotations) and Corinne gets everyone manipulating a model of the proposed office extension. Your first impressions are confirmed.

If you communicate using V, H and F, you dramatically increase the likelihood that true learning will take place.

VHF in language patterns

Before applying this learning to your course design, you need to know that there is another way of identifying VHF preferences. It is by noticing language patterns.

Derek habitually uses expressions like:

> ❍ 'We need to get to grips with this problem.'
> ❍ 'We want to stir things up a bit here.'

What do you think his preference is – V, H or F?

Eva habitually uses expressions like:

> ❍ 'I like the look of this proposal.'
> ❍ 'I can see what you mean.'

What do you think her preference is – V, H or F?

Fergal habitually uses expressions like:

> ❍ 'I think we're in tune on this one.'
> ❍ 'Sounds pretty good to me.'

What do you think his preference is – V, H or F?

Even when they are just speaking, people often give an indication of their preferred way of thinking. Further examples of V, H and F language patterns are given below.

EXAMPLES OF LANGUAGE PATTERNS

Words and phrases that people use when in visual mode

> ❍ 'I see what you mean.'
> ❍ 'I can picture that.'
> ❍ 'have an insight'
> ❍ 'focus on . . .'
> ❍ 'vision'
> ❍ 'I'm looking closely at the idea.'
> ❍ 'We see eye to eye.'
> ❍ 'Show me what you mean.'
> ❍ 'It colours his whole attitude.'
> ❍ 'I'll take a dim view of it.'
> ❍ 'This will shed some light on the matter.'

Words and phrases that people use when in hearing (auditory) mode

- ○ 'I like the sound of that.'
- ○ 'Let's discuss . . .'
- ○ 'Listen to . . .'
- ○ 'rings a bell'
- ○ 'I don't like your tone.'
- ○ 'on the same wavelength'
- ○ 'in harmony with'
- ○ 'a lot of mumbo jumbo'
- ○ 'loud and clear'
- ○ 'calling the tune'
- ○ 'in a manner of speaking'

Words and phrases that people use when in feeling (kinaesthetic) mode

- ○ 'I don't like the feel of it.'
- ○ 'I feel good about that.'
- ○ 'scratch the surface'
- ○ 'That's rough.'
- ○ 'I can't grasp it.'
- ○ 'I'll keep in touch.'
- ○ 'a cool customer'
- ○ 'falling to pieces'

So how can you apply this VHF concept to your training course? Remember, if you want to communicate powerfully, use words and phrases that appeal to all three modes. If you want learning that really sticks, engage people in activities that use all three ways of thinking.

A VHF makeover

BEFORE THE VHF MAKEOVER

Here is a section from a training course on coaching skills.

Set up
Trainer: An important part of coaching is to help the other person to know about their goals. Good questions to ask are 'What do you want?' and 'How will you know that you've got it?'. What I want you to do is to get into small groups and discuss typical answers that you might get to those questions when you are coaching your staff.

Activity
Participants discuss in groups.

Set down

Trainer: Any comments or questions on that exercise?

A desultory discussion follows.

As you will have noticed, this whole activity appeals mainly to the hearing mode. Here's a revised version.

AFTER THE VHF MAKEOVER

Set up

There is a big colourful picture on the flipchart of a football whizzing in to a goal.

Trainer: An important part of coaching is to help the other person to be really clear about their goals. If you don't know where you're going, it's unlikely that you will ever get there. I'm going to ask you a couple of questions – you don't have to answer them out loud, but I want you to notice how you feel when I ask them. Question one is 'What do you want from your job?' [pause] Question two is 'How would you know that you've got it?'. [pause] Interesting questions! You might find these questions exciting or scary but you'll certainly experience something, and that's because goals are important.

What I want to do is to demonstrate asking these questions in a coaching context [turns over flipchart to reveal the two questions]. After that, you're going to have a go and see for yourselves how it works. I need a volunteer. [Demonstrates how to ask the questions] Now get into pairs. Take five minutes each to explore with the other person their answers to these two questions. Help them to see themselves in a new light.

Activity

Participants work in pairs.

Set down

Trainer: Here's my trusty beanbag. When I throw it to you, catch it and then tell us what you've learned from the last exercise. When you've shared the learning, throw it on to a person of your choice, and then it's their turn to be under the spotlight.

As the participants comment, the trainer summarizes the points on a flipchart which is later displayed in the training room.

At the end the trainer says: 'I can see that you've really got a good grasp of how to ask these questions in a really powerful way.'

Activity: VHF makeover

List all the different ways in which the second version of the training course excerpt appeals to visual, hearing and feeling modes.

Visual	Hearing	Feeling

In most groups, it is likely that there will be a mixture of preferences. The figure below gives several ideas on how you can engage (or 'grab') everybody.

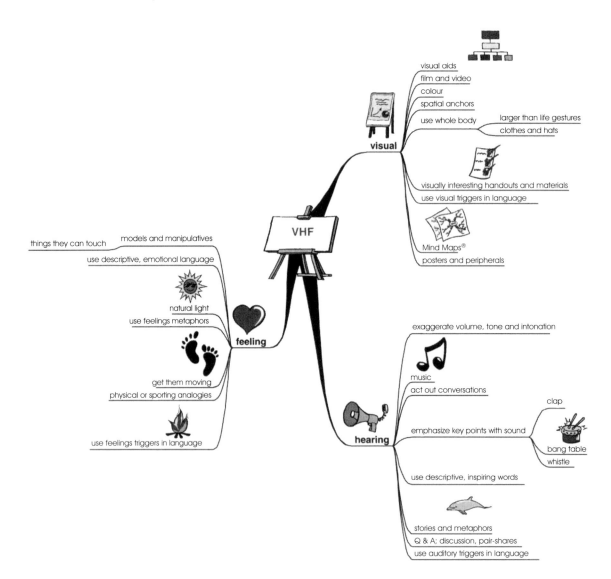

32 Magical metaphors

Years ago, a friend cooked some Chinese food for Kim and she was struggling a bit with the chopsticks. Finally, the friend said: 'Just pick up one chopstick and hold it like a pencil. Move it around a bit like you would with a pencil. Now slide in the other chopstick between the base of your thumb and the top of your fourth finger and keep it still.' Bingo! Kim was suddenly using chopsticks. The key to success was a simple metaphor – hold it like a pencil – which enabled her to relate new learning to existing learning.

Different kinds of metaphor

As well as aiding learning, metaphors help us to explore various ways of thinking about things. Different metaphors can illuminate different aspects of a situation. In a wonderful book called *Images of Organization*, Gareth Morgan[22] explores how different metaphors about organizations help us think differently about organizational development.

One of the most common metaphors for an organization is a machine: 'I'm just a cog in a big machine.' If you think that an organization is a machine, how would you try to improve it? By stripping out and replacing worn or defective parts? By ensuring everything was measured so that it fitted exactly into place?

On the other hand, if you thought an organization was like an organism, how would you try to improve it? By ensuring it was well nourished and got enough exercise? By healing any parts that appear to have been injured?

Different kinds of metaphor lead us to different insights – so choose your metaphor carefully.

Course themes

You can extend a metaphor to cover the whole of the learning experience. For example, on our courses on brain-friendly learning we sometimes use the metaphor of 'training is like being at the beach'. It's lots of fun, and can be invigorating and high-energy, as well as very relaxing and rejuvenating. We reinforce this metaphor – this theme – by decorating the room with starfish, parasols, shells and kites.

Activity: What is a metaphor?

Identify suitable metaphors to help a person to learn the following skills:

1. Riding a horse

2. Explaining the difference between hardware and software on a computer

3. Listening to someone really carefully

4. Building trust with a colleague

5. How we want to treat our customers

There are an infinite number of responses to this activity; here are some of them.

1. Riding a horse is a bit like driving a car. When you're learning you have to concentrate hard to do everything properly, but after a while it becomes automatic.
2. Computer software is like some pencil notes on a page – although it carries important information, it's easy to rub it out and start again. The hardware is like the paper the message is written on – it's there for good.
3. Being a good listener is like being a good lover – everyone thinks they can do it, although few people realize how much skill is involved.
4. Trust is like fine porcelain – it takes a long time to make and is easily broken.
5. We tend to think of our customers as if they are cattle coming to be milked – we herd them into the shed, do the business and herd them out again. What about if we treated them like thoroughbred racehorses, who need to be groomed carefully if they are to give of their best?

33 Stories and anecdotes

The next step on from a simple metaphor is an anecdote or story. Stories are an incredibly powerful way of learning. Think for a moment about some of the most influential teachers throughout history – Confucius, Jesus, Mohammed, Gandhi. How did they get their message across? Was it by issuing policy statements? Did they fire up a PowerPoint presentation and talk people through a list of bullet points (with the odd spreadsheet thrown in for extra excitement)? No they did not. What they did was tell stories. In fact, great contemporary communicators use much the same strategy – they tell lots of stories.

Stories can be short, almost snippets:

> Good morning – welcome to this course on customer care. I almost didn't get here this morning, because when I arrived at the university car park this morning, the security guard told me that the car park was already full. But when I explained that I had a course to deliver in just a few minutes, he telephoned one of his colleagues and arranged for me to park in the yard, which as you probably know is usually reserved for the executive. That's what I call good customer service!

Stories can be longer:

> Let me tell you about the event which convinced me that all this rapport stuff really works. Kim and I had pitched for a piece of work with a large company. We'd been invited to a final meeting with the board before they decided whether or not to go ahead. We knew that most of the board was pretty keen with the exception of Hugh, the financial director. Kim was leading the meeting and I didn't have a great deal to say or do. I decided to turn all my rapport skills on to Hugh. I mirrored him exquisitely – his posture, his gestures, even his breathing. It's about twenty minutes into the meeting and Hugh is talking about some team-building issues in the finance department. Then he says, 'Why don't we ask Larry to come in and do a team-building session before we begin the main project?' I was astounded – not only was Hugh meant to be the one with reservations about using our consultancy firm, but he was asking me to lead the session – the only person at that meeting who'd hardly said a word! But, non-verbally, I'd been building rapport with Hugh to the extent that he felt he could trust me – such is the power of mirroring.

Stories can be funny. The chairman of a large company found that his car wouldn't start. He telephoned the car pool to see what else was available:

> An enthusiastic voice answered the phone, 'Car pool.'
> 'Car pool?' said the chairman. 'What have you got down there?'
> He replied, 'We've got vans for going to and from the factory. We've got Mondeos for the sales reps. We've got BMWs for the directors. And we've got a big fancy Mercedes for Fatty, our chairman.'
> The chairman said, 'Do you know who this is?'
> He said, 'No.'

I said, 'This is your chairman.'
Long pause.
Finally, he said, 'Do you know who this is?'
The chairman said, 'No.'
He said, 'So long, Fatty.'

Stories can be true:

A reporter asked the English football team coach, 'Has the defeat by Portugal made you rethink your position on tactics?'

'Oh yes mate,' came the reply, 'I'm definitely thinking of using tactics in future.'

Stories can be made up:

A shepherd was herding his flock in a remote pasture when suddenly a brand new Range Rover emerged from a dust cloud travelling towards him. The driver – a young man in an Armani suit, Gucci shoes, Ray Ban sunglasses and a Hermes tie – leaned out of the window and asked the shepherd, 'If I can tell you exactly how many sheep you have in your flock, will you give me one?'

The shepherd looks at the young man, then at his peacefully grazing flock and calmly answers, 'Sure!' The yuppie parks the car, whips out his notebook, connects it to a cellphone, surfs to a NASA page on the Internet where he calls up a GPS satellite navigation system, scans the area, opens up a database and some 30 Excel spreadsheets with complex formulae.

Finally, he prints out a ten-page report on his hi-tech miniaturized printer, turns round to our shepherd and says, 'You have here exactly 1586 sheep!'

'That is correct. As agreed, you can take one of the sheep,' says the shepherd. He watches the young man make a selection and bundle it in his Range Rover.

Then he says, 'If I can tell you exactly what your business is, will you give me my sheep back?'

'Okay, why not,' answers the young man.

'You are a consultant,' says the shepherd.

'That is correct,' says the yuppie. 'How did you guess that?'

'Easy,' answers the shepherd. 'You turn up here although nobody called you. You want to be paid for the answer to a question I already knew the solution to. And you don't know a thing about my business because you took my dog.'

Human beings love stories. Stories have the ability to address both explicit, conscious learning and implicit, unconscious learning, simultaneously. What stories can you gather, glean or devise?

Activity: Looking for stories

Spend an hour with a pile of newspapers, watching TV news channels or surfing news stories on the Internet. What stories can you find which have a relevance to some learning event you will be facilitating?

Activity: Brew a great training story

1. Find a story, incident, or 'slice of life' that had an impact on you.
2. Mentally rehearse telling the story.
3. Let it settle in – at least overnight.
4. Recall it again and notice the major themes, associations, metaphors and potential lessons in the story.
5. Let it settle in again overnight.
6. Link the story to the content of your session.
7. Tell the story – realizing it will grow and change each time you tell it.

As well as telling single stories, it can be useful to tell stories in nested loops – in other words, put one story inside another one. For example, *Alice in Wonderland* is really just a simple story about a girl who falls asleep, has a dream and wakes up again. But nested inside this story is another story, which is the story of her dream – everything that happens down the rabbit hole. Nested inside this story are a number of other stories – for example, the story of the Walrus and the Carpenter.

Stand-up comedians use a similar technique. They will begin to tell a story and then go off at a tangent and tell another story, before coming back to complete the first story. You can use this technique to great effect as a facilitator of learning. Here's the basic structure with three stories:

- ❍ Tell the beginning of story A.
- ❍ Run activities around topic A.
- ❍ Tell the beginning of story B.
- ❍ Run activities around topic B.
- ❍ Tell the beginning of story C.
- ❍ Run activities around topic C.
- ❍ Conclude story C.
- ❍ Conclude story B.
- ❍ Conclude story A.

This is a particularly satisfying and rich way of using stories to enhance learning experiences.

34 Unconscious learning

No, this does not mean learning while you are asleep! But, because much of the way in which your brain learns is beyond conscious awareness, learning which accesses your unconscious mind is the most powerful learning of all.

Yet, is there really an unconscious part of your mind? Consider these examples.

If you drive a car, do you consciously make a decision to brake, steer or change gear? Probably not – these tasks are handled out of conscious awareness.

Any task which requires rapid and precise motor movements – playing a musical instrument, touch typing and many sports – is performed too rapidly to be controlled consciously. Of course, it's still being orchestrated by our brain – but by the unconscious part of our brain.

When you hold a conversation with someone, are you consciously planning which words to say and how to arrange them so that they all come out grammatically correct? Again, no – you may consciously plan the overall meaning of what you are going to say (and, then again, you may not!) but the precise and rapid linguistics are all handled out of conscious awareness. In fact, the more you think about it, the more astonishing the process of speech is. Not only do you not have to think consciously about which words to use, you don't have to think about which muscles to move to get your tongue, mouth and vocal cords in exactly the right configuration to produce the right sound. All that, too, is handled out of conscious awareness.

When you begin to learn a new skill, you may have to think about it consciously. Can you remember when you first learned how to drive a car? You needed a great deal of conscious effort to begin with. Then the more you practised, the easier it became, until it became almost completely automatic. This is true of most skills; at the outset, you learn them consciously and, with practice, they become automatic. To put it another way, they become a habit.

You can increase the power of any learning event by addressing the unconscious mind as well as, or instead of, the conscious mind. One way to do this is by the use of embedded commands.

Consider the example below.

Example: Embedded commands

Can you remember a time when you were working (playing?) with a group and it felt like there was magic going on? Whether you have or haven't experienced this kind of training magic yet, you have some way of knowing, at a deep level, that **you are capable** of this kind of elegance.

You have your own way of doing things, and that's just perfect – and I know that you are reading this manual primarily to **learn how to be an even better facilitator**. I don't know how you'll realize you can **master these skills**, but I do know that you will **use them ethically and effectively** to help people learn what it is they most want to learn.

But what's far more important, really, is to appreciate the enormous power of **your unconscious** mind and the way that you can **learn new things effortlessly and easily** – to know that you can demonstrate exactly what it is that you most need, in the exact way that will be most helpful, exactly when you choose to.

And even more important than that is to **appreciate who you already are** – with all the skills and capabilities that you already have. You can **appreciate yourself** for having invested the time and energy in developing skills that not only grow you but also **grow other people**. How many people can you help to grow in a lifetime? You'll only know after it happens. Until then you can **look forward** to it, and just **focus on enjoyment** of the process.

An embedded command is an instruction, which is interpreted differently by the unconscious mind than it is by the conscious mind. For example, if you say to someone. 'It's good to be in a place where people like to **have a great time**', and you use a slightly different tone of voice for the words '**have a great time**', this is what will happen. Your listeners' conscious minds will register the whole sentence, but their unconscious minds will register the instruction **have a great time** and act accordingly.

Here are a few more examples. Imagine hearing the sentences set out below with a slight emphasis on the words in bold. Can you see how your **unconscious mind will get** it, even if your conscious mind isn't able to **think differently**?

❍ To **be honest** with you, this next activity is open to all sorts of approaches but, to **be frank** with you, you'll get the most out of it if you **take it seriously**.

❍ Some people like to **participate fully in this activity** and some people are not so sure about whether to **participate fully** – do what works for you.

❍ You may be thinking to yourself, how can I **get the best out of this event**? Maybe I should take lots of notes, maybe I should **ask lots of questions**. Maybe I should just **stay open to new ideas**.

○ I need someone to **volunteer now** for this role-play. Don't feel **you have to volunteer** – I only want a **volunteer** so that everyone **can learn a lot today**.

If you are thinking to yourself, 'I never use embedded commands', consider this: every time you say to someone 'Don't **do that**!' you are giving an embedded command. The conscious message is, of course, 'Don't do that'. However, in order for the brain to process the instruction 'Don't do that' it has to form an image of whatever 'that' is. In so doing, the message to the unconscious brain – the embedded command – is to do it! That's why if you say to a child who is carefully walking with a full glass of water 'Don't spill the water!', you can practically guarantee that they will. Never say to anyone 'Don't do that!': instead, tell them what you do want them to do – 'Walk carefully', for example.

In other words, **give instructions positively**!

Activity: Embedded commands

Think of a learning event you will be facilitating in the near future. Consider the introduction you normally give to this event. What do you normally say, and how do you say it? Now rephrase your introduction, to include one or two embedded commands. If you want to **have lots of ideas**, reread the section above.

Frequently Asked Question

Q: Isn't this a bit manipulative – giving people commands that only their unconscious is aware of?

A: You are continuously addressing the participants' unconscious minds. Almost every time you open your mouth you are giving an embedded command – which may not necessarily be very helpful. For example, a trainer who says 'Don't **worry about today's training** – most people don't **find it as boring as it sounds**' may not know about embedded commands, but he is certainly sending a powerful and unhelpful message to the learners. Given that you are doing it anyway, isn't it better to **be aware of what you are doing**, so that you can **use it ethically and in the interests of the learners**?

35 Mnemonics

 Colours of the rainbow? Richard Of York Gave Battle In Vain gives you red, orange, yellow, green, blue, indigo, violet.

Ten intelligences? Loveable Lads In India Make Very Bad Noodles Every Evening.

The notes on the lines of the musical treble clef? Every Good Boy Deserves Favour gives you E, G, B, D, F.

Orders of precedence in the British nobility? Did Mary Ever Visit Brighton Beach gives you duke, marquis, earl, viscount, baron, baronet (especially useful if you are suddenly made an earl and you are not quite sure where to place yourself in a procession behind the Queen).

Better still are the kind of mnemonics where the initial letters spell a word in themselves. For example,

HOMES gives you the Canadian great lakes – Huron, Ontario, Michigan, Erie and Superior.

 Frequently Asked Question

Q: This isn't making it easier – it's even more work to have to learn the mnemonic too.

A: It works because remembering anything unusual is much, much easier than remembering things which are ordinary and commonplace. Try it and see.

36 Rhythm and rhyme

Complete the following phrases:

1. Thirty days hath September, April, June and . . .
2. Mary had a little lamb, its fleece was white as snow; and everywhere that Mary went, her lamb was . . .
3. One o'clock, two o'clock, three o'clock rock
   four o'clock, five o'clock, six o'clock rock
   seven o'clock, eight o'clock nine o'clock rock
   We're gonna . . .

The answers are, of course, 'November', 'sure to go', 'rock around the clock tonight'. What makes it so easy to remember these phrases? Repetition plays a part – certainly, in the case of the nursery rhyme, you probably repeated it as a child many, many times. This is less likely to have been the case with 'rock around the clock' unless you are a Bill Haley fan. What all three have in common is rhythm and rhyme. It is this quality that makes them memorable.

Here are some ways in which you can incorporate rhythm and rhyme into training:

 ○ incorporating simple rhymes into learning points: One trainer we know is very keen on encouraging participants to move around during learning events. He sums up this belief with the phrase: 'If your body don't move, your brain don't groove.'
 ○ getting participants to invent songs or raps to sum up learning.

37 Humour

Humour makes a big difference to training and learning. It is a great state changer. Even when people are feeling lethargic or low, humour has the ability to put them into a better state almost instantly.

As humour engages the emotional centres in the brain – which help memory creation and retention – it can often make learning points more elegantly and powerfully than a more serious presentation.

Humour is also a great way to build rapport. If you can get a group to laugh, you are well on the way to building rapport with them (that's assuming that they are laughing with you, rather than at you, which is a different strategy altogether).

Laughter also strengthens the immune system. People who laugh a lot tend to stay healthier and deal with stress more effectively.

So do you want the good news or the bad news?

Here's the bad news. Some people are naturally very funny and others are not. We both know trainers who, with apparently no effort at all, have course participants rolling in the aisles with uncontrollable gusts of laughter. We also know trainers who, with no special preparation, are able to be deadly serious for hours on end. Not everyone is naturally funny.

Now the good news. Everyone can use humour in training if they want to. But, by humour, we don't mean telling jokes. There are many different ways of using humour in training, and we'll look at a selection here. Choose the methods you feel most comfortable with and prepare your own selection of humorous interventions. One word of warning about this section: good humour doesn't always transfer from live action into the printed word – sometimes you have to have been there. So if some of these strategies don't seem all that funny on the page, take it from us that they all worked well at the time.

Examples of humorous interventions

THE UNEXPECTED TWIST

The trainer introduces a course on creative problem-solving by quoting that familiar proverb: 'A problem shared is a problem doubled.'

UNEXPECTED LINKS

Just as the trainer is saying 'This is a very important point', the fire alarm goes off. The trainer continues, 'So important that we all need to walk out to the car park right now and think about it some more.'

ALLUDING TO THE PROCESS

A participant says, 'One of the problems we senior managers have is that we tend to repeat ourselves.'

The trainer responds, 'So you said earlier.'

It's a course on time management. The trainer says, 'Do any of you have a problem with procrastination? Would you like to learn a really good technique for dealing with it? We'll learn how to deal with procrastination on this course . . . if we get around to it.'

It's a course on coaching skills. The trainer is making the point that when people ask questions in a coaching session, they often already know the answer. One of the participants asks, 'Would that be true even when you are working with inexperienced graduates?' The trainer pauses and says, 'I believe you already know the answer to that one.' Some moments later when another participant asks another question, the trainer merely has to give a quizzical look for everyone to laugh.

CATCHPHRASES

'It's goodnight from me and it's goodnight from him.'
'Nice to see you, to see you . . . nice.'

These phrases are not particularly funny in themselves, but repeated often enough by people on television, they become funny (well, slightly funny anyway).

Often, courses spontaneously develop their own catchphrases – or you can promote them.

UNUSUAL METAPHORS

'That's like asking turkeys to vote for an early Christmas.'

INSULTING THE PARTICIPANTS OR THE ORGANIZATION

Trainer: 'Now this next exercise is on emotional intelligence. Now I know that, because you're all accountants, you view emotions as at best irrelevant and at worst dangerous, but just bear with me – you might find this interesting.'

QUOTATIONS

'As Groucho Marx once said, "I'd never want to be a member of any club that would have someone like me as a member".'

FINALLY

Using humour is largely about being in the right state, and creating perfect rapport with the group.

Activity: Your humour

Review the list above. What kinds of humour do you currently use when you are training? What kinds of humour could you use?

38 Breaks

Breaks are important in learning – everybody needs them for refreshment and they can provide a natural 'punctuation point' in the flow of the session. They are also a useful additional device for managing state, and give a great opportunity for the participants to build one-to-one rapport with other learners and with you.

There is a basic physiological rhythm in our day governed by our automatic and endocrine systems. This basic rest–activity cycle (BRAC) lasts about 90 minutes, and it's a good rule of thumb to have a break every hour and a half or so, or do something which reduces the pace for a while.

Breaks also helps learners integrate the material – our unconscious mind keeps processing and creating new connections even when we're stood around chatting about something entirely unrelated to the learning event.

To make the best use of breaks:

- ❍ Break at a high point wherever possible – this anchors good feelings to the session.
- ❍ Provide brain-friendly snacks (especially fruit) and encourage people to drink lots of water.

Pre-break rituals

It's a good idea to create rituals just before a break, to enhance group rapport and to capitalize on primacy and recency. Here are some ideas for pre-break rituals.

COLLECTIVE SINGLE CLAP

Ask the group to stand in a circle and put their left hands out in front of them, palms up. Remind them that everything they came in with still counts – all their knowledge, experience, wisdom and skills. Ask them to mentally create a representation of all these things in their left hand. Keeping their left hands out, ask them to stretch their right hands out behind them, and look back over their right shoulder. Tell them that in their right hand is a representation of all the new things they are learning, and give them a moment to visualize that. Then, ask them to bring their right hand down on to their left hand in a single clap on the count of three, thus integrating everything they came in with with everything new in a way that is totally resourceful, appropriate and ethical. In a group that is in rapport, the single clap is literally that – everybody makes the sound at precisely the same moment.

COCKTAIL PARTY QUESTIONS

Have the group wander round the room, pretending to be at a cocktail party. As they approach each new person, ask them to answer a question or complete a statement that you've already posted on the flipchart, or that one of them has suggested. Alternatively, just have them tell each other three ways in which they are going to apply what they have learned back in the workplace.

PERIPHERAL WANDER

Ask the group to wander slowly around the room (perhaps provide some background music) absorbing the peripherals and posters, and to absorb whatever meanings emerge. Alternatively, ask them to choose a favourite to share with a buddy or the whole group after the break.

GROUP BALL THROW

The participants throw a soft ball around and, as each person catches it, they answer a question, such as 'What's been the most significant thing for you in the last session?' or 'An idea I can use immediately is . . .'. A variation is for each person to think up a new question just before they throw the ball to somebody else.

OR YOU COULD . . .

- ❍ Have some brain gym with some anchored theme music.
- ❍ Reshow key visual aids, perhaps with background music.
- ❍ Hold a concert review (either by you, or one of the participants).

After the break

A small, but important, factor is how you instruct the group when to be back. Say 'We'll start promptly at 11.15' rather than 'Let's take a ten-minute break'. Many people won't bother to 'synchronize' their watches, and you'll get stragglers unless you specify an exact time.

If the whole group isn't back on time, start anyway. If it's really important that everybody is there before you introduce the next activity, have something for people to do in the meantime – for example, a relevant crossword or quiz, another cocktail party question, or just quiet reflection, either individually or with a buddy on how they are progressing towards their learning goals.

Tools for managing state

39 Positive expectations

Why positive expectations matter

Do you know what a self-fulfilling prophecy is? The term first came into use in 1930s America. A number of people were predicting that the banks would run out of money. When they heard this, a lot of customers went to the banks and withdrew their cash and lo and behold – the banks *did* run out of money. Sometimes just thinking something can make it true.

The classic experiment on self-fulfilling prophecies in the world of learning was carried out, also in America, in the 1960s. Robert Rosenthal and Lenore Jacobson[24] told teachers that a testing programme had identified a particular group of students as having unusually high potential. A year later the high-potential group had gained more than 15 IQ points above the normal group. In fact, the so-called high-potential group had been chosen entirely at random – the increase in achievement was a self-fulfilling prophecy.

The self-fulfilling prophecy can work in the other direction too. Research in the 1990s by Renate and Geoffrey Caine[25] showed that students perform better when they perceive the teacher to have expertise and to be committed to their learning. The key word here is *perceive*: two teachers who, in reality, have equal expertise and are equally committed will get different results if their students perceive one to be more expert and committed than the other.

What are the implications of all this for facilitators? First, have positive expectations of what the participants on your courses can and will do. Second, create positive expectations of your expertise and commitment to caring for the participants.

Creating positive expectations

PRE-COURSE MATERIAL

Where appropriate, let people know that this event has already been run a number of times and that people have enjoyed it and learnt a lot.

Also, give some information about yourself and other facilitators on the event, which demonstrates your expertise and commitment to participants.

YOUR INTRODUCTION TO THE EVENT

Reinforce the message about previous runs of this course and your expertise and commitment. It may be helpful to ask someone else to introduce you – it's easier for someone else to blow your trumpet!

DURING THE EVENT

Continue to build your reputation as someone who has expertise by:

- ○ working without notes
- ○ using anecdotes which illustrate your expertise
- ○ quoting accurate numbers, dates and names
- ○ referring accurately to the latest research in your subject
- ○ alluding to news and current affairs in relation to your subject
- ○ including information about yourself and your expertise in the course handouts.

Continue to build your reputation as someone who is committed to participants by:

- ○ arriving early and greeting people
- ○ using participants' names
- ○ talking to people during the breaks – in particular, following up with individuals who have raised particular points during the session
- ○ giving participants your e-mail address or telephone number and encouraging them to call you after the course is over.

Activity: Summarizing your expertise

Identify a training event you will be leading. Assume that someone else will be introducing you. Prepare a short introduction for them to read out about you.

Activity: Learning names

Here's an infallible way of remembering people's names.

Create an association between the person's name and their physical appearance. The more outlandish the association, the easier you will find it to remember.

On the following page are eight photographs of individuals, together with their names. Use the strategy of creating an outrageous association between their names and their appearance. Some suggestions of associations are given for you below but, if you can think of your own, so much the better. Once you have matched these eight faces and names, turn the page and write in each person's name below the picture. Remember, the pictures will be in a different order over the page.

Luther Daley   **Nico Antonio**

Richard Woodley   **Suzi Yue**   **Tom Grindlay**

Angela Keaton   **Stacey Martin**   **Ellie Harding**

Luther Daley. Imagine him sitting on a toilet (*loo*) rubbing his moustache. Instead of using toilet paper he tears off the date page from a day calendar and he does this every day (*daily*).

Nico Antonio. Look at his thick black hair. Now imagine that, instead of it being slicked back as in the picture, it is hanging down in front of his eyes because he has just got out of bed. He starts to shave but *nicks* himself in the process. When he looks to see what he has done all he can see is a big *ant on* his face.

Richard Woodley. Imagine him as a very *rich* man; his glasses are made of pure silver and his crutches are made of gold. Now imagine him hobbling on his crutches into the *wood* and *lay*ing down under the trees.

Suzi Yue. Imagine this little girl is with you in court; she is *suing you* for the damage you caused to her lovely uniform.

Tom Grindlay. Think of a big *tom* cat nuzzling against that shaggy white beard (or link Tom's face to another person you know called Tom). Now imagine him *grind*ing his teeth on the end of the pipe and then see him *lay* it down on a fence in front of him.

Angela Keaton. Concentrate on the wispy tendrils of hair falling around Angela's face and then slowly imagine her transform into an *angel*. Now imagine her trying to carry the *key* to heaven but she just can't manage because it is too heavy – it weighs a *ton*.

Stacey Martin. Look into Stacey's big brown eyes; they have a faraway look. She is lost and has asked you to help her. You tell her to *stay* here and wait until she *sees* you coming back (exaggerate the actions you would use, as if she didn't understand you). She just gazes straight ahead, so you turn to see what she is looking at and behind you is a huge bird – a house *martin*.

Ellie Harding. Invent your own associations, for the practice!

Now match the names to the faces on the following page. We bet you get Ellie Harding right – it's your association!

You can use this strategy in different settings. Some trainers like to greet people as they arrive, ask them for their names, and then use the association strategy to remember the names. Alternatively, you can wait until everyone is seated, and ask them to introduce themselves. As they do so, write down everyone's name on your own seating plan. While the participants are engaged on their first activity, use your seating plan and the association strategy to memorize everyone's names.

Once you have learnt the names, use them frequently. You will find that, after you have used a name two or three times, you will no longer need to use the outlandish association to recall it. The name will just be there.

Frequently asked questions

Q: What if I make my outlandish association based on the person's clothing, and they wear something different on the second day of the course?

A: No problem. The association is just to get you to remember the name in the first place. Once you have memorized the name, and have used it two or three times, you will no longer have to use the association.

Q: Aren't some kind of associations well, you know, a little disrespectful?

A: Fair point, and if you feel uncomfortable with a particular association, use another one that you do feel comfortable with. But the truth is that the more outrageous the association, the easier your brain will remember it – and you can still treat the person with genuine respect.

Q: Can't I just read their name badge every time?

A: Well you can, but that does nothing for your credibility and commitment to the participants. But I'm glad you mentioned it, for this reason; sometimes people's 'official' name on their company ID badge isn't the name they wish to be called by. Be sure to address people by the name they prefer, not just the one on their tag.

Activity: Creating positive expectations

Identify a course you will be delivering. List below some actions you can take to create participants' positive expectations of you.

1. Before the course:

2. At the beginning of the course:

3. During the course:

40 Rapport

Why rapport matters

One of the most significant differences between a successful facilitator and an unsuccessful one is the ability to develop rapport with a group of participants. Think of a very positive experience you had as a participant on a training course. Now think of the person leading that course. They almost certainly came across as knowledgeable in their subject area, but this in itself is not enough – we can all think of people who are great experts in their chosen field but are terrible teachers. They almost certainly had a range of interesting training techniques at their fingertips, but, again, this is not enough – we can all think of people who have all the techniques but who are still not great facilitators of learning. When you think of a great teacher or trainer, the chances are that they also possessed that something extra – that ability to really understand the needs and desires of the participants. That 'extra' is what we call rapport.

When we are in rapport with another person, we usually experience a feeling of mutual trust – a sense that we are warming towards the person, even if we do not know them that well. This feeling puts us in a very positive and resourceful state for learning. As a result, we have very positive expectations for what we will learn, which in turn makes it more likely that we will have a positive learning experience. It is a virtuous circle.

Building rapport with participants is one of the facilitator's most important tasks. This section shows you how.

Building rapport through words

One of the most straightforward ways of building rapport is through words.

○ **Acknowledge participants' interests and concerns.**
Take the trouble to find out about the participants so that your introductory comments can build rapport.
○ **Acknowledge participants' jargon and in-jokes.**
Almost every group has its own jargon and in-jokes. Referring to these in an appropriate way builds rapport.
○ **Use relevant language and metaphors.**
If you are working with a group of engineers, use engineering language and metaphors; if you are working with a group of artists, use artistic language and metaphors.
○ **Refer back to participants' comments.**
Use phrases like 'And as Mary mentioned earlier, it's very important to . . .'.

○ **Use personal disclosure.**
   Share something personal about yourself – take the risk of opening
   yourself up as a whole person, not just as a trainer.

Activity: Course makeover

Identify a course you will be leading. List various rapport-building phrases you could use to achieve the objectives below:

○ Acknowledging participants' interests and concerns

○ Acknowledging participants' jargon and in-jokes

○ Using relevant language and metaphors

Building rapport by matching body language

Imagine, for a moment, the scene in a candlelit restaurant. You are enjoying a delicious meal, and you notice in the far corner of the restaurant a couple who are obviously deeply in love and enjoying a romantic evening together. They have complete rapport with each other. What do you notice about their body language?

Well, when people are in rapport they tend to adopt very similar body language. You might notice this with the romantic couple. When she leans forward, he leans forward. When he pushes his chair back a little to relax, she does the same. When she takes a sip of wine, he does too.

Now change the scene to your staff canteen. This time the food is not so delicious, but you can still watch people across the crowded room. At one table, the man is sitting very upright and talking in quite a loud voice. Across the table, his partner is slouched into a very relaxed position and looking a little dreamy. Are they in rapport? Probably not. But at another table, where both people are sitting in a very relaxed position and talking in a similar tone of voice, the chances are that they are in rapport.

None of these people has had any training in building rapport. It just happens naturally. You can learn from their experience. If you want to build rapport with people, one of the quickest ways is to adopt similar body language. You match your body language to theirs. Here are some of the aspects of body language you can match.

1. General body posture:
   – upright or slouched
   – distribution of weight.
2. Arms:
   – crossed or uncrossed
   – position – on chair, in pockets, supporting face and so on.
3. Legs:
   – crossed or uncrossed
   – tapping or still
   – contact with floor.
4. Voice:
   – tone – high, medium or low
   – speed – high, medium or fast
   – tonal variation – monotone or lots of variety.
5. Breathing:
   – rate – fast, medium, slow
   – location – upper chest, lower chest, abdomen.

Let's say you want to build rapport with participants on a training course (and you do). When you are talking to them one-to-one, it is easy – you simply match appropriate aspects of their body language. What about building rapport with a whole group? Here are some pointers.

Are there common patterns repeated throughout the group? If most of the group are sitting back in their chairs and looking very relaxed, you can build rapport by sitting back too. On the other hand, if they are all sitting up very straight, you can build rapport by matching their posture too. I once ran a morning session for a group of PR people who were very high-energy and fast-paced, followed by an afternoon session with a group of university professors who were very laid-back and slow-paced. In order to maintain rapport with both groups my morning session was very energetic and feisty whereas my afternoon session more reflective and measured.

Sometimes you may want to build rapport with an individual in a group setting. For example, it can be very useful to change your body language to match the person in the group who happens to be speaking at the time. This demonstrates that you are really listening and valuing their comments. Matching body language is even more useful if you want to disagree with someone. If you tell someone that you disagree with them (in a pleasant and respectful way, of course) and continue to match their body language, you will most probably continue to stay in rapport with that person. The individual concerned will stay in a positive state, and can continue to learn on the course.

Frequently asked questions

Q: Do you mean to say that if I mimic every gesture that another person makes it will help me to get in rapport with them? Surely they would be irritated if every time they do a nervous cough I do the same?

A: The key to rapport is matching, not mimicking. You should adopt a similar posture, not mimick every single idiosyncrasy. Matching works best when it is not picked up by the other person's conscious awareness.

Q: Isn't this all a bit manipulative? Getting someone to like you by copying their body language?

A: Matching body language to build rapport is a natural process – we all do it anyway when we feel in rapport with someone. All you are doing here is speeding up what would most probably happen anyway. But rapport is just a tool and, like any tool, it can be used for good or for ill. You match body language in a manipulative way if you chose to, but we hope you will use it in a positive way, to enhance your participant's learning.

Q: What if I can't match the person's body language? What if the person is talking in a deep voice and crossing their legs, and I have a naturally high-pitched voice and my clothing prevents me from crossing my legs?

A: No problem – you don't have to match everything. What about matching their general body posture, or speed of voice instead?

Activity: Building rapport through body language

Think of a person you don't get on with very well, but with whom you have fairly regular dealings – a work colleague perhaps. Think about the last time you met with them. Now complete as much of the following table as you can, based on what you remember from that meeting. First complete the column for the other person. When you have finished, complete the column for you.

	Them	You
General body posture Upright or slouched Distribution of weight		
Arms Crossed or uncrossed Position – on chair, in pockets, supporting face etc		
Legs Crossed or uncrossed Tapping or still Contact with floor		
Voice Tone – high medium or low Speed – high medium or fast Variation – monotone or lots of variety		
Breathing Rate – fast, medium, slow Location – upper chest, lower chest, abdomen		

You may not have been able to complete every box, either for them or for you. That's OK – but try to notice these things next time you meet.

For the boxes you *have* completed, what differences do you notice between their body language and yours? Now identify just one or two things that you could do differently next time you meet, in order to match their body language a little more and build rapport. List your action points below.

Action points

Next time you meet, match their body language in the ways you have listed and notice the difference!

Pacing and leading

The ability to build rapport quickly with a group of participants on a training course is one of the most useful skills for any facilitator. But can you have too much rapport?

Let's say you are leading a training event for a group which is low-energy and dispirited. Obviously, you don't go bouncing into the group, full of the joys of spring, telling them about this absolutely wonderful learning experience that will change their lives forever. This approach would not put you in rapport with the group. Instead, you might begin the course in a more gentle way, acknowledging the difficulties the group have been facing. But if, at the end of the training event, you have matched the group so exquisitely that they are still feeling dispirited and low-energy, you have probably missed something.

A really skilful facilitator will first build lots of rapport by matching the group and acknowledging their concerns. Once they have sufficient rapport to build trust, they will then lead them into a more resourceful state. This technique is known as pacing and leading.

Here's an example of pacing and leading in the training context.

Example

A facilitator is engaged to do a training session on team briefings. She arrives to find a group of participants who view team briefings as a totally unnecessary extra burden on already hard-pressed team leaders. The participants look tired and lethargic.

To begin with, the facilitator is fairly low-key. She acknowledges the pressures the group is under, and recognizes that they may feel that team briefings are unnecessary. She helps them explore some of the problems and difficulties the team leaders are facing in their job. For the first hour or so of this one-day training session, her focus is on building rapport with the participants.

After a morning break she has built sufficient rapport with the group that they are now open to learning more about team briefings. She engages them in some activities, which involve group work and movement, and the energy level begins to rise. She lets some of her enthusiasm for team briefings show, and the participants start to get quite interested in the topic.

By the afternoon, the participants know that they can really trust this facilitator. She gets them to prepare and act out some role-plays of team briefings, and, by now, the energy level is high and the participants are fully involved in the learning. At the end of the day the participants are reluctant to leave.

You could say that, for the first part of the morning, the facilitator was pacing the group. Only when she had established good rapport did she lead them into new territory. If she'd entered the training room super-enthusiastic about team briefings, the participants could have dismissed her as yet another naïve trainer full of 'management speak'; conversely if she had merely paced them all day she might have left them as cynical and lethargic as they'd started. In this case, she got the balance just right.

How do you know when you have done enough pacing and it is time to lead? To some extent, this is down to experience – try it and notice when it works. Being alert to people's body language gives you some useful clues – do people look as if they are ready to move on?

Activity: Pacing and leading

Recall a training event you have experienced, which began with participants who were wary and sceptical, and which ended with them being enthusiastic and having learned a lot. You may have been at this event either in the role of participant or facilitator. Now, jot down your answers to the following questions:

1. What did the facilitator do to gain rapport with the group?

2. At what point in the day did the facilitator move from pacing to leading?

3. What do you consider the key to this event's success?

4. What could the facilitator have done to have made it even more successful?

What rapport really means – entering the other person's world

Let's imagine that we have been to see a play together. When we compared notes afterwards, would our experience of the play have been identical? Unlikely. Even if we shared broadly the same experience of the play – that is, we both liked it or we both didn't – we probably noticed different things. I liked the set design; you thought the sound effects were particularly interesting. You thought that one of the actors almost forgot his lines at one point. I didn't notice this, although I was particularly struck by the fact that this actor bore an uncanny resemblance to my Uncle Dave. And so on.

As with the theatre, so with life. Each of us experiences life in our own unique way. Not only do we notice different things, but we attribute different meanings to things. If I spill a drink I find it funny; someone else spills a drink and flies into a rage. Spilling a drink tells me that gravity still works; someone else spills a drink and that tells him that he is a clumsy oaf.

We all have our totally individual versions of the world as we perceive it. The miracle isn't that people sometimes don't communicate. The miracle is that people ever manage to communicate at all! So what's all this got to do with rapport or brain-friendly learning?

In essence, rapport is being able to enter another person's individual world – or at least come close to it. And making the effort to understand another person's world is one of the greatest compliments you can pay them. Essentially, you are saying to them that their world is worth noticing. Whether you do it through words, or through non-verbal means, you are acknowledging their world and their uniqueness and value as a human being. And that's why rapport is so important.

41 Flow

University of Chicago professor Mihalyi Csikszentmihalyi has spent his life researching why people do what they do.[26] He has studied thousands of people engaged in challenging activities – such as rock climbing, dancing and chess – as well as leading teams, performing surgery and composing music. What made these activities enjoyable? He found that the most rewarding aspects of these challenges are:

○ designing something new
○ discovering something new
○ exploring new places
○ solving problems
○ learning something new.

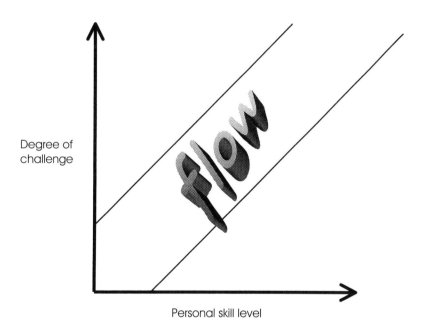

How can Csikszentmihalyi's work help you as a facilitator? Put simply, you want a flow state in your learners – you want to present them with a challenge that transforms learning from a chore into an adventure. How quickly can you facilitate this state, and then get out of the way? Flow brings automatic state management, intrinsic motivation, and joyful, natural learning. The secret is not to rely on carrots and sticks to motivate people, but to provide them with unique opportunities to discover, learn and grow.

High challenge and low stress

A significant part of your brain will ensure that survival needs dominate – especially when a threat is perceived. In such circumstances, creativity is set aside in favour of quicker, more tried and tested behaviours. Survival always overrides pattern detection and problem-solving. When someone is in distress, you can expect very constricted, predictable behaviour patterns – a 'ghost' of their true potential.

Computer-generated images show this clearly. Under perceived threat or in distress:

○ adrenaline is released into the bloodstream
○ heart rate speeds up
○ blood flow and electrical activity alters to 'minimize' brain activity
○ cortisol is released (small amounts feel good but higher amounts depress the immune system, tense the muscles and impair concentration).

Continued moderate to high distress exposure:

○ releases glutocortoids that severely inhibit attention
○ results in extreme confusion and poor distinctions due to increased amounts of cortisol.
○ kills neurons in the hippocampus (the area of the brain that helps us 'package' learning into long-term memory). You literally 'lose your mind'!

In the modern training context, distress and threat rarely come from a sabre-toothed tiger entering the training room! However, threat can be perceived from any of the following:

○ potential physical harm, unacceptable risk levels
○ intellectual threat
○ derisive comments, put-downs and sarcasm
○ social embarrassment
○ reward/punishment systems
○ isolation from peers
○ being 'set up' or 'patsied' by facilitators or colleagues
○ constricting time deadlines
○ resource restriction.

Your goal is to create a learning environment free from distress and threat, whilst keeping challenge high.

Activity: Being in flow

List at least four occasions when you were truly in a flow state – doing anything, not necessarily in training context:

1.

2.

3.

4.

List at least three occasions when participants on a training course you were facilitating were in flow.

1.

2.

3.

List at least two things you did that helped to create a flow state.

1.

2.

List at least one thing you can do to create more flow on learning events you facilitate in future.

42 Let's get physical

Why physical activity helps learning

How do children learn to walk? Is it by quietly listening to a talk from their parents about human balance and locomotion? No, it is by trying to walk, falling over and trying again. How many times do they try? As many as it takes.

Now, while it's pretty obvious that you can only learn to walk by doing it, in fact children learn most skills this way. Central to a child's learning experience is movement and action. Even when they are learning factual information, children learn more easily when they move about.

Throughout most of history, movement and action have been central to learning. People have learnt to talk, cook, plant seeds, gather hay, tend herds, build, make furniture, print and tan leather by being around someone who already has that skill and copying them.

In fact, the whole reason that humans and other animals have a brain and nervous system at all is because they move. Plants don't have a brain or a nervous system – they manage very well without, thank you very much – but if animals didn't have a nervous system and a brain, however rudimentary, moving around would be tricky, to say the least. Movement and learning are inextricably linked.

So, if you think about it, it's very curious that we should accept the notion that learning in a classroom or training room often involves people sitting down in the same position for long periods of time. It may be administratively convenient for the teacher or trainer, but it does nothing for learning.

What happens when people remain seated for any length of time? Typically there are two physiological responses. First, there is a drop in the level of oxygen in the bloodstream, and hence in the brain. Although the brain represents only 3 per cent of our body weight it uses 25 per cent of the oxygen. In fact, brains are just crazy about oxygen. Most brain scanning techniques rely on the fact that when an area of the brain becomes active, it uses more oxygen, and so the blood flow to that part of the brain increases.

The other response to sitting still for too long is a drop in the level of adrenaline in the brain. Adrenaline is a chemical which signals our brain to stay alert and active. When our adrenaline levels drop too low, we go into a mild trance and learning more or less grinds to a halt. When training, have you ever experienced that sinking feeling that accompanies the realization that you are talking and hardly anyone in the group is really paying any attention? Perhaps in that after-lunch slot popularly known as the trainer's graveyard? Well, what has almost certainly happened is that your participants' oxygen and adrenaline levels have dropped so much that they're not physiologically able to pay attention to anyone. The quickest way to change state? Introduce some movement! Oxygen and adrenaline levels automatically rise when people start to move, and you can restore people to that resourceful learning state.

Easy ways to incorporate movement

IN THE TRAINING ROOM

- ○ Ask for a show of hands.
- ○ Do an activity standing up.
- ○ Encourage applause.
- ○ Get participants to change seats or location.
- ○ Change groups.
- ○ Take a break.
- ○ Go for a walk.

IN LEARNING DESIGN

Learning activities

All the following learning activities incorporate movement:

- ○ introductory activities
- ○ mapping and drawing activities
- ○ simulations
- ○ treasure hunts
- ○ role-plays
- ○ energizers.

Energizers

You don't need to do any energizers at all; in fact there's much to be said for structuring your training using learning activities which naturally incorporate movement. However, there will often be occasions when an energizer is appropriate – when energy levels are flagging, or when you feel a need to change the group state. As a rule of thumb think in terms of using two or three energizers each training day.

Some people love energizers and would happily do nothing else all day! They are good fun, and the movement generally gives people a sense of well-being. On the other hand, there are others who find them 'embarrassing' and a distraction from 'the real learning'. In our experience, these people are in a minority, but nevertheless this is how they feel. So how do you tackle this dilemma as a facilitator?

The answer is to pace, pace, pace and lead. Start off with energizers that are short and not too outrageous – taking a stretch or equilateral triangles maybe. Then move on to more lively activities. Be very positive about encouraging people to join in, but also give them the opportunity to opt out if they wish. It may also be helpful, in some circumstances, to explain why you are using energizers. You will usually find that with an appropriate degree of pacing, even people who are initially reticent actually come to enjoy them!

Two good resources for energizers are:
Icebreakers, Andy Kirby (ed.), Gower, Aldershot, 1993, ISBN 1 85904 044 6.
Icebreakers 2, Michéle Barca and Kate Cobb, Gower, Aldershot, 1993, ISBN 1 85904 037 3.

Activity: Let's get physical

Identify a course you will be delivering in the near future. Jot down, on a separate sheet of paper, an outline of the various sessions.

Refer back to the list under 'Easy ways to incorporate movement – in the training room'. Choose one or two examples that would be appropriate for this event and include them. Amend your session outline accordingly.

Refer back to the list under 'Easy ways to incorporate movement – in learning design'. Use one of the ideas from this list to redesign one of the sessions on your course. Amend your session notes accordingly.

Refer back to the list under 'Energizers'. Choose two or three which would be appropriate to the group and the event. Amend your session notes accordingly.

43 Brain gym

What is brain gym?

The pattern of activity in your brain has a direct impact on your physical body. When you perceive that your arm is itching, the physical sensation you're aware of isn't happening in your arm at all – it's happening in your brain. This is why people who have lost limbs often experience itching or other sensations in their 'phantom limbs'. The limb itself may have gone, but the part of the brain which used to control that limb is still there, and can still experience a range of sensations.

If brain activity can have a direct impact on your physical body, it follows that your physical body can have a direct impact on your brain activity, and this, in a nutshell, is the basis of brain gym. Certain physical movements have an effect on the way your brain operates. Understanding the exact physiological mechanism isn't that important. Most people seem to experience benefits from taking part in the short physical activities described below. You can use them as stand alone energizers, or you can combine them together into an energizer of your own invention. One trainer we know gets course participants to follow him doing a fabulous sequence of movements which incorporate many of these activities, to the music of James Brown. Feel free to improvise!

Six activities

CROSS CRAWL

With your right hand, touch your left knee. With your left hand, touch your right knee. Repeat. You can do it to music and move around the room as you do the movements. For extra energy you can use your right elbow to touch your left knee and so on.

What are the benefits? Apart from generally increasing energy by introducing a little movement, the cross crawl integrates the left and right sides of the brain, making for more creativity and better concentration.

THE ELEPHANT

Imagine that you are an elephant, with big ears, a long trunk and strong legs planted firmly on the ground. Lay your ear against your shoulder and reach out your arm like a trunk. Swing your arm, head and the top half of your body loosely through the air as if you are drawing a huge figure 8 on its side. Do this two or three times with each arm.

This exercise relaxes neck muscles and enhances listening and balance.

GRAVITY GLIDER

Stand up, cross your legs and relax your knees a little. Let your head and body hang forward. Slowly swing your head and upper body from left to right, two or three times. Then come up, cross your legs the other way and repeat.

This activity is good for spatial awareness, visual concentration and self-esteem.

BRAIN BUTTONS

Open out one hand and place it on your upper chest, just below the collar bone. Use your thumb and finger to rub your 'brain buttons' – soft spots just by your collar bone. By a process similar to acupuncture, this helps to increase your visual acuity. At the same time, rest the first and middle fingers of your other hand on your belly button and think pleasant thoughts.

POSITIVE POINTS

Just between your eyebrows and your hairline are two slight mounds on your forehead. These are your 'positive points'. Gently massaging these points will help you release stress, improve memory and feel good. Better still, get someone else to massage your positive points.

COOK'S HOOK UPS

This exercise is done in two parts. First, sit on the floor and put your left ankle over the right one. Next, extend your arms and cross the left wrist over the right. Then interlace your fingers and draw your hands towards your chest (some people will feel more comfortable with the right ankle and right wrist on top). Sit this way for one minute, breathing deeply, with your eyes closed and your tongue in the roof of your mouth. During the second part, uncross your legs and put your fingertips together, continuing to breathe deeply for another minute.

After this, you'll feel relaxed, energized and attentive.

Activity: Brain gym

Choose one of the brain gym activities listed above and incorporate it into a forthcoming training event. Be sure to practise the activity yourself several times so that you feel completely at ease with it.

44 Music

Music and learning

Music's reputation as the universal language is certainly well-deserved, and recent studies are increasingly indicating the benefits of music in the learning situation.

One of the founding fathers of accelerated learning, Dr Georgi Lozanov[27] observed that: 'a well-executed concert can do about 60% of the presenting work in about 5% of the time'. Why? Because music activates the limbic system, so that the learning is much more likely to be encoded into long-term memory. Music has the unique quality of integrating the emotional, cognitive and psychomotor elements that activate and synchronize brain activity.

Evidence from schools shows that not only is the study of music beneficial in itself, but the introduction of music into any learning situation also causes a marked improvement in maths, sciences and reading.

Hideo Seki of Tokyo used music to teach a course on electricity and magnetism to his computer science students. The first day was devoted to goal-setting and positive suggestions by and for the learners. The rest of the programme was sequenced as follows:

- ○ ten minutes of mood-setting music as the learners arrive
- ○ presentation of new material by means of a lecture with no music
- ○ new material presented visually with an overhead projector – with more active music and learner involvement
- ○ the same material presented with slow, instrumental music, with the learners just listening
- ○ energizing music as the learners leave.

At the exam, three times as many students than in previous classes achieved scores better than 80 per cent.[28]

Well-chosen music leads to:

- ○ relaxation and stress reduction
- ○ fostering of creativity through brain wave activation
- ○ stimulation of motor skills, language and vocabulary
- ○ better class discipline, and group rapport
- ○ increased attention span
- ○ settling of hyperactive learners
- ○ a more focused and aligned group
- ○ improved long-term retention and memory.

The pulse of the body (heartrate) tends to synchronize (entrain) with the beat of the music, so choose different beats depending on the effects you want to create. For example, slower, baroque music can slow down the pace of a workshop, allowing learners to focus.

Mozart's music has been causing particular excitement amongst researchers. At the Center for the Neurobiology of Learning and Memory at the University of California's Irvine campus, students listening to Mozart for just ten minutes prior to taking a SAT test raised their scores by an average of 9–12 points! Control groups listened to other music or studied in silence.[29] Other studies have shown that listening to Mozart whilst studying measurably increases learning, memory and reasoning.

Choose music carefully – depending on your desired outcome. Don't just choose music that you like (although this will, at least, keep you in a great state).

Musical/rhythmic is one of the intelligences identified by Howard Gardner – see 'Multiple intelligences' at page 135.

Uses of music

- ❍ as a call-back 'anchor' after breaks or group activities
- ❍ as a state changer or energizer
- ❍ in active learning concerts (see page 205)
- ❍ in passive learning reviews (see page 206).

You can choose music to:

- ❍ **energize** – wake up, prepare for performance, recharge
- ❍ **relax** – manage stress and anxiety, learn patience and people skills, meditate, speak more freely
- ❍ **focus** – enhance intellectual performance, facilitate memory and learning, prolong attention span
- ❍ **uplift** – break bad moods, escape from negative thought patterns
- ❍ **cleanse** – vent feelings of frustration, anger and grief, handle problem relationships
- ❍ **create** – solve problems, access right-brain imagery, innovate.

For a detailed discussion on how to choose music to create the above states, see our 'Further resources' on page 226.

What kind of music and why?

Whilst you don't have to become an expert on brainwave patterns to successfully introduce music into your learning events, it's useful to understand the basics about why certain kinds of music should be used in different situations. Look at the table below showing the relationship between brain rhythms and beats per minute (of the heart, or of the music).

Brain state	Rhythm of brainwaves	Heart/pulse/beats per minute of music	How it feels
Delta	0.5–3 cps	Resting rate	Deep, dreamless sleep, no outer awareness
Theta	4–7 cps	Resting rate	Unconscious, light sleep, deep meditation
Alpha	8–12 cps	60–80 bpm	Aware, relaxed, calm, high suggestibility, daydreaming
Beta	13–40 cps	80+ bpm	Normal waking, consciousness, alert, active

Note: cps = cycles per second; bpm = beats per minute.

The alpha state is excellent for learning facts, synthesizing new knowledge, strengthening long-term memory, and nurturing creativity. It's interesting to note that the rhythm of ocean waves, as with music at 60-80 bpm, can stimulate alpha brainwaves in some people. Perhaps that's why we find the ocean so relaxing.

As a general rule, use slower and quieter music for reviews (around 60 bpm) and faster and louder music for activities (around 80 bpm).

Types of music for 'sound surfing'

STATE CHANGERS AND ENERGIZERS

Your playlist for these needs to change in line with changes in contemporary and popular music and in line with the age and preferences of your group. Watch out for copyright issues (see 'Mind your Mechanicals' on page 207).

PREVIEW

Use 'preview music' for three to seven minutes just before and during the initial interview. Depending on the theme, content of the session and the state you wish to create, this could be light, fun and attention-getting or dramatic and uplifting. You could also use movie or TV advertisement themes, music from shows, from pop, rock or New Age music.

ACTIVE CONCERT

For detailed content, speak over a background of instrumental music. Let the music play first for between 10 and 30 seconds, then just join in – don't compete with the music. Use the pauses in the music. Pause during very loud or active parts. Reading or speaking with music is a skill, like any other, that needs to be practised. Tape yourself, and listen to the results. Get to know the rhythm of the piece of music you'll be using. See 'Further resources' on page 226 for resources that will help to develop this skill.

Choose classical (c. 1750–1825), romantic (c. 1820–1900) or New Age instrumental music or, alternatively, use music that was deliberately composed to lift the spirit (for example, Handel, Vivaldi, Corelli, Bach or Pachelbel).

The ideal pace is 70–80 bpm.

PASSIVE REVIEW

For a passive review of the day or session (that is, one where the learners are just relaxing and reflecting) choose pieces characterized by soothing strings – for example, violins, guitars or harps. Avoid brass or horns, which have lower frequencies and can sound too abrupt and intrusive for generating an alpha state. Many people find the experience more powerful if they close their eyes – but it isn't mandatory! Aim for 60–70 – the baroque style of music (c. 1600–1750) works well.

Introducing music for concert previews and reviews

Start by playing alpha music during team and individual exercises. If this is new for people, give minimal explanations of the research supporting it. Turn the music down if the learners complain. You'll find that most learners don't notice it after a short time – which is what you want. You will notice an increase in energy levels, retention and enthusiasm.

Some learners in the corporate world may feel uncomfortable closing their eyes for a passive review – at least initially. Indeed, this technique may be inappropriate in certain settings and, as a facilitator, you need to respect this. Where appropriateness is an issue, we sometimes use passive concert reviews which combine background music with watching a visual presentation – perhaps a repetition of overheads or flipcharts used earlier in the day.

For variation ask the learners to take turns in reading the material to each other, using music as a background, or have the group create an active concert review from written material or Mind Maps® and perform it for each other.

Too much music creates saturation. Aim to use it for 30 per cent or less of the training time (unless you're teaching a music class).

OTHER TIPS

Avoid music that is very well-known as it may trigger memories in learners that are undesirable. One of Kim's favourite pieces of joyful music is Pachelbel's *Canon in D Major*, but, unfortunately, it was played at Princess Diana's funeral. This is a real shame, because now some people comment that it triggers memories of sad times for them, and therefore hinders learning.

If possible, place your music source so that it is closest to the left ears of your learners. More research is needed on this, but there is some evidence that the effects of sounds heard by the left ear are more easily translated into the right hemisphere of the brain.

We are grateful to Dr Mark McKergow for permission to include the following piece which explains clearly and concisely all you need to know about music copyright. Dr McKergow is an independent scientist and consultant specializing in maximizing the effectiveness of learning and training in organizations. He is also a saxophonist, and ran the modern jazz orchestra UltraSound with support from the Arts Council of Great Britain. He imports CDs designed for use in the training room from sources including Tune Your Brain, Mozart Effect and the LIND Institute. His website address is www.mckergow.com.

Mind your Mechanicals!

Licensing issues relating to music in the training room.
The legal situation regarding using recorded music in public differs between the USA and the UK. ('Using music in public' is legal terminology, and includes running training courses, even if they are in-house events and not 'public' by the customary definition.) These notes relate to the United Kingdom.

In the UK, the rights to use recorded music are policed by the Mechanical Copyright Protection Society (MCPS). Do not confuse MCPS with the Performing Rights Society (PRS) who monitor live performances of music. MCPS issues licences for the use of recorded music in a huge variety of circumstances – in films and TV, in advertisements, on records and in shopping centres. Outside of film, TV etc. they issue licences which relate to the premises rather than the music. This means that, in general, buildings either have licences to use recorded music or can get them. Many hotels, conference centres etc. already have such licences. All schools are covered for music used during classroom lessons by a blanket MCPS licence.

If your building does not have a licence, another route is by becoming licensed as a 'mobile DJ'. This allows you to use any legitimately purchased CDs, tapes and records in any place (subject to other by-laws – so no raves in your back garden, then). Using your own recordings of other people's CDs is out – but if you're into that you'll hardly be reading this. The mobile DJ licence cost £126.20 plus VAT in 2000, and can be obtained by calling the MCPS licence hotline on 0800 0684828.

The UK is, I venture, much better off than the USA where every piece of music seems to be individually licensed. There are a number of sellers specializing in CDs which are either royalty-free (which can sometimes seem quality-free too), or who sell you the rights to use their music in with the price.

Mechanical Copyright Protection Society Ltd (MCPS)
29-33 Berners Street
London W1T 3AB

Tel: 020 7580 5544
Fax: 020 7306 4455

Licence Hotline: 0800 0684828

45 Nourishing the brain

The purpose of food and drink is to supply the body with the raw materials it needs to function. As with any production facility, the outcome or end product that we desire depends on the raw materials that we use.

One of the principal raw materials the body needs is in the form of various amino acids, available in different types of food. They are important for learning because they stimulate neurotransmitters in the brain. Different amino acids stimulate different neurotransmitters, so, in order to affect our state, we need to know which neurotransmitters we need to trigger and then work out which amino acid will do the job. Use the diagram below as a simple guide.

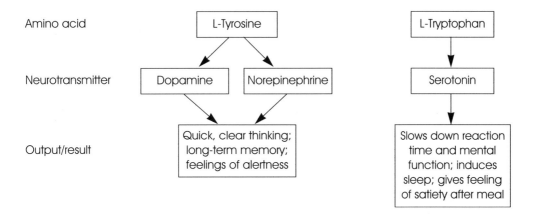

Foods to encourage learning

As you can see, the foods you should eat while learning are those that contain L-Tyrosine. These include:

- ❍ nuts
- ❍ beans and peas
- ❍ lentils
- ❍ cottage cheese
- ❍ soy products
- ❍ fish and seafood
- ❍ poultry
- ❍ eggs
- ❍ meat.

Preferably, foods should be organic to avoid toxicity from chemicals, which may have an adverse effect on the brain – this is especially important for meat and poultry.

It is also important to stimulate the neurotransmitter acetylcholine for memory. For acetylcholine to be produced we need oxygen (exercise and abdominal breathing) and glucose, which is the main fuel for the brain. (However, it should be noted that all foods eventually break down into glucose!) Fruit and vegetables are an effective way of providing a quick conversion to glucose; they are also an important source of anti-oxidants, which work to destroy harmful substances in the body.

WATER

It is very important to keep the brain hydrated if you want to feel alert. The brain is around 80 per cent water and is one of the first parts of the body to be affected by dehydration resulting in loss of concentration, fatigue, slow reactions and stress. Under normal circumstances our bodies need two litres of water per day to maintain a properly hydrated state. This increases when we are in situations that cause perspiration – for example, in a warm environment and during exercise.

In order to hydrate the body, water should be sipped slowly and frequently. Drinking quickly is like throwing a whole bucket of water on a patch of dry earth – some is absorbed but most of it just runs off and is wasted. Be guided by your thirst as well as quantity. If you are thirsty you are already dehydrating, and thirst should never be ignored. If you get a headache try sipping two large glasses of water before reaching for the painkillers; often this is just another warning sign that the brain is dehydrated.

Foods to avoid

Referring back to the diagram on page 209, you will realize that it's best to avoid foods that stimulate serotonin whilst learning. These are pasta, potatoes, bread, milk and bananas. These are great foods for after your learning session when you want to relax and unwind but should be avoided if you are skipping the afternoon siesta!

It is also important to avoid stimulants, depressants, highly refined sugars and food additives. Although drinks such as coffee and tea may initially make you feel more alert, they act as a diuretic and will leave you dehydrated and cause stress when the effect starts to wear off. If you are a high consumer of these drinks start to reduce your intake slowly. Caffeine is a powerful drug and stopping it instantly will result in withdrawal symptoms.

Caffeine, alcohol and sugar also have the effect of reducing dopamine levels in the brain, and therefore reduce alertness, the ability to think quickly and clearly and the transfer of learning into the long-term memory.

Last but not least, avoid overeating. Digestion uses a considerable amount of energy and processing power. Once food is inside the body, the body must use resources in order to process it. If there is a large amount of food to digest the body will divert energy from other functions in order to complete this task. This is why some religions use fasting as a means of encouraging spiritual enlightenment – it encourages clear thinking.

A typical brain-friendly buffet

○ Snacks – crudités and dips, fresh fruit
○ Salmon parcels (poached salmon in bite-sized pieces wrapped in a lettuce leaf)
○ Oat cakes or rice cakes spread with tahini, hummus, guacamole or cottage cheese
○ Bean stew with brown rice
○ Chicken skewers (alternate pieces of chicken and vegetables threaded on a wooden skewer)
○ Salads – green leaf salad, pepper salad, tomato, cucumber and black olive salad
○ Baked apples, grilled fruit with natural yoghurt, fruit salad
○ Rye pancakes filled with assorted berry fruits topped with crème fraiche
○ Nuts and dried fruit

46 Anchoring

What is anchoring?

If you do your shopping in a large supermarket, you will probably be familiar with the smell that greets you when you go in the door; it is the aroma of freshly baking bread. Smells have a powerful effect on state. Most people, when they smell the aroma of freshly baked bread automatically feel very comfortable and homely – and hungry. If you think about it, this is exactly the state that the supermarket would like you to be in when you visit its store. They certainly want you to feel good, but they are also quite happy for you to feel a little bit hungry, because people who feel hungry usually buy more. (Recall an occasion when you went shopping for food just after a heavy meal – you were probably disinclined to buy very much.) That's why supermarkets go to considerable lengths to ensure that the smell of baking bread wafts over the entrance door, even if the in-store bakery is the opposite end of the building.

The smell of baking bread triggers a state of well-being and hunger. We call this an anchor. In this context, an anchor is anything which reliably produces a state or action in another person. Some anchors are pretty universal. Certain kinds of music produce, in most people, a state of mild anxiety, which is why they are featured in Hollywood films just before our hero is about to be attacked by a rampaging mob wielding chainsaws, machetes and tactical nuclear devices! Other anchors are more idiosyncratic. Do you have a piece of music that you associate with a time you were in love? This music may mean nothing to the population at large, but whenever you hear it you go into a sentimental, romantic state.

Anchors are all around us. They can be:

- ○ **Visual**: is there a certain picture or piece of scenery which is guaranteed to send you into a particular state?
- ○ **Auditory**: do certain kinds of music trigger a certain state for you/?
- ○ **Kinaesthetic**: what about the feel of getting into crisp, freshly laundered bed sheets, or the feel of a hug from a loved one?
- ○ **Olfactory**: what does the smell of frying bacon do to you?
- ○ **Gustatory**: do certain kinds of food consistently produce a certain state? Chocolate for instance?

So, what's all this got to do with brain-friendly learning? Effective learning takes place when the learner is in a resourceful state. Anchors consistently send people into certain states. It follows, then, that if you know how to use anchors, you can ensure that people are in a resourceful state for learning. To do this you need to know something about how anchors are created.

Creating an anchor

There are basically two ways of creating an anchor. The first is by habituation. If you consistently associate a given stimulus (the anchor) with a given response, then the stimulus alone will trigger the given response. Does the name Pavlov ring a bell? On a training course, play the same piece of music consistently just before calling people back from a break. You'll only need to do it once or twice and then, as soon as you put the music on, people will start to return to the training room.

When you are delivering some input to a group, stand up. When it's time for a group discussion, sit down. Again, having done this a few times, people will naturally fall silent when you stand, and begin to engage in discussion when you sit down.

The other way to create an anchor is to associate the stimulus and response just once, but in a highly emotional way. People who have had a flaming row in a particular office will often feel anxious whenever they go in that office because that single, negative emotionally charged experience has created the sight of that office as a negative anchor. People who once had a very romantic meal in a particular restaurant will often feel good when they go there, because that single positive emotionally charged experience has created the sight of that restaurant as a positive anchor.

If you are using role-play on a course it can be very effective to perform the role-plays in a different room, or a different part of the main room. Role-plays often have an emotional content, and participants quickly learn to associate being in the role-play with a particular location. Being in that location helps them to get into the right state for role-playing; moving out of it helps them get out of role and learn from the experience in a more detached way.

There is more information on anchoring in the figure below and also in Tools 47, 48 and 51.

Some useful anchors to create

Purpose	How
Making a clear distinction between input of information and group discussion	Facilitator standing means information input; facilitator sitting means group discussion.
Keeping a discussion on track	Have the topic of the discussion written up on a flipchart; when the discussion goes off-course stand and point to the flipchart.
Reconvening after a break	Always use the same piece of music to call people back after the break
Making a clear distinction between different kinds of facilitator input	Standing at one side of the room means 'get ready for some humour'; standing at the other side means 'here's some serious input', standing in the middle means 'listen carefully while I give you instructions for the next activity'.

Purpose	How
Animating a story	Use different voice tones and stand in different positions to mark out the different characters in the story.
Making a clear distinction between different facts or approaches	Use different voice tones and positions.
Encouraging people to be in a state of curiosity	Ask questions like 'Have you ever wondered what it would be like if . . .'.
Making a clear distinction between different kinds of activity	Move to a different part of the room to do certain activities – for example, role-plays.

Finally, it's worth remembering that people come to learning events with a whole collection of anchors already set up. Consider for a moment what images and associations most people conjure up when they think about attending a training course. For people who have not done much training, the nearest association they can make is with attending a class at school – and, for many people, this may not have been a particularly pleasant experience. So, with no effort at all on your part, the mere mention of a training course is enough to send people into an unresourceful state.

It's part of your job to create some new positive anchors associated with learning and training.

Activity: Anchoring

1. Identify, and note down in the space below, a particular training event you will be facilitating.

2. From the table above, choose two anchors that it would be appropriate to use on this course.

3. Write down specifically how, when and why you will be using them.

47 Existing anchors

You already have thousands of anchors that trigger different states – some resourceful, some less so. When you think about it, the entire advertising industry is built on the idea of anchors. Advertisements are designed to create 'good' states (for example, sexy, powerful, safe, healthy) in us and then link these states to the product.

Activity: Discover your anchors

What are some of your anchors? Write down one example for each of the five modalities.

Type	Anchor (trigger)	State or feeling
Visual (seeing)		
Auditory (hearing)		
Kinaesthetic (feeling)		
Olfactory (smell)		
Gustatory (taste)		

Activity: How would you rather feel?

What state do you typically have in the following situations and what state would you ideally like to have?

Situation	Current State	Desired State
Facilitating or training		
Exercising		
Handling routine domestic chores, such as shopping, cleaning or ironing		
Giving somebody critical feedback		
Travelling to work		
Arriving home at the end of the day		
Meeting new people		

Give yourself a new anchor for any of the above situations in which you would like to be more resourceful.

By the way . . . do you realize that **you** are an anchor? You trigger states in others simply by your presence in a group. You cannot avoid influencing people in one way or another. What kind of anchor do you **want** to be?

48 Installing your own anchors

Anchoring: the definition

Anchoring is the process of associating an internal response with some external or internal trigger, so that the response may be quickly re-accessed. Anchoring can be visual (looking at a specific picture), auditory (by using specific words and voice tones, hearing a specific piece of music), and kinaesthetic (as when touching a particular part of the body).

How to anchor a state

1. **Identify** the state you want to anchor (for example, confidence).
2. **Access** the state by fully associating back to a time when you felt totally confident. Really go back and relive the experience intensely. If you feel you have never in your life experienced total confidence, that's still OK! Just imagine it –.guess – or step into the shoes of the most confident person you know, even perhaps a fictional character or somebody you've never met. The important thing is to make the experience associated as intense as you can. Step out and break state. Re-access the state a few times until you are sure that you can intensify it and know when to time the peak moment!
3. Just as the state is peaking, **introduce your anchor**. This can be a visual representation, a word or phrase said in a particular tone, a piece of music, or a particular touch or gesture. Repeat this process a few times, making sure that you keep or intensify the feelings and the associated physiology (that is, what you are doing in terms of your posture, gestures, facial expression and breathing).
4. Break state. Test your new anchor by recalling the mental picture, the word or phrase or piece of music, or by gesture or touch – whichever you have chosen. Feel yourself enter the desired state.

Activity: Make an anchor collection

Develop a shopping list of anchors that you could use in everyday situations. Check that they meet the criteria for effective anchors:

○ They are precise.
○ They are easily reproducible.
○ They can be used uniquely to anchor specific states.

49 Learning from criticism strategy

Have there been times when your state has slipped, because somebody, or a group of people, said something you perceived as 'critical'? It's probably happened to all of us at one time or another.

The ideal scenario is to maintain a resourceful state, at the same time extracting the useful learning from the criticism. A useful 'belief' to hold about criticism is that it always has a positive intention behind it – namely, to coach you to be even better – even if the critic is unskilled, sarcastic, or just downright rude and offensive!

Neuro-linguistic programming (NLP) offers a very useful process (developed by Steve and Connirae Andreas)[30] and set out in the activity below. It's a good idea to mentally rehearse this strategy a few times, so that you can automatically begin the process the next time anybody criticizes you – either publicly or privately.

Activity: Learning from criticism strategy

People who deal extremely well with criticism typically do two things: they detach themselves from any bad feelings – and they evaluate the criticism whilst feeling resourceful. Practise the following strategy to help you achieve this state.

1. Think back to a time when somebody criticized you – to your face. Choose a 'mild' criticism to practise the strategy, and then you can go on to more challenging incidents!
2. Imagine yourself now behind a plexiglass screen – you can see and hear what's being said, but the criticism cannot penetrate. Safe behind this screen, see yourself on the other side of it and just allow yourself to decide what the criticism means to you. The 'you' over there is having to deal with it. The safe 'you' here can just listen in a neutral state. Just trust that you know how to do this really well. Run the entire episode through in your mind, like seeing a video of what happened.
3. Now, still safe behind your screen, clarify what the critic means. Ask some questions of the critic, from a curious state of mind, but without any bad feelings. Check what the critic would have wanted you to do differently – this may be useful. It doesn't mean you have to change your behaviour, but it's important information.
4. When you have enough information, compare your memory of the event with the critic's version. How well do they match? What are the significant points of difference? What was your outcome? What was theirs? How well did you achieve your outcome?
5. The 'you' in front now gets to choose an appropriate response:
   – You could agree with the criticism.

– You could apologize.
– You could ask for support in changing.
– You could offer your version of the 'truth'.
– You could tell them what your outcome was.
– You could disagree and tell them why.
– You could do nothing – and perhaps choose to discuss it at another time.
– You could use it to make a learning point with the whole group.

6. Have the 'you' over there now rehearse the response they have chosen. See and hear them giving this response, and have them rehearse until it looks and sounds congruent and comfortable. Coach the other 'you' on what else might improve the behaviour – for example, appropriate body language or tonal emphasis.

7. When the response is entirely congruent, allow the screen to dissolve and join up again with the other 'you'. Integrate what you have learned.

50 Changing the state of the group

Here's a smorgasbord of strategies for influencing the state of groups you work with:

❍ Remember a time when ... (re-access the state from the past).
❍ Go into the desired state yourself and then lead.
❍ Tell a story which evokes the state.
❍ Use your voice tone.
❍ Do something that evokes the state naturally.
❍ Ask them to move or use their bodies in a way that creates the state.
❍ Ask directly.
❍ Ask indirectly – use embedded commands.
❍ Create an imaginary context – 'as if' ... .
❍ Give them a task.
❍ Fire a previously installed anchor.
❍ Use a pattern interrupt – that is, create an unexpected intervention that interrupts the current patterns of feeling, thinking and behaving. Good ideas are: to suddenly inject humour (have the group divide into pairs and tell their partner the most corny joke they know); ask a completely irrelevant but empowering question (for example, 'How good do you really want to feel right now?'); make a loud noise (for example; bang on the flipchart or table, play a snippet of music) to snap people into a different state; have the group improvise a different state to interrupt a pattern that is not desirable. However, only use these strategies if you have exquisite rapport with your group.
❍ Play music.
❍ Ask them how they would prefer to do it!

What other ideas can you generate?

Activity: State changers

Think of three states that would be distinctly unhelpful in the groups you work with. Make these real examples if you can, or consider a few 'nightmare' scenarios! For example:

○ bored and cynical
○ resentful, sarcastic or angry
○ low-energy
○ anxious.

You can use the list of states on page 223 if you wish for ideas.

Now think of the states you would rather the group was in – in order to optimize their learning and enjoyment. So, now you have some transitions, such as:

○ cynical ——————▶ excited
○ low energy ——————▶ energized and vibrant
○ anxious ——————▶ adventurous and unstoppable!

Knowing what you now know about changing states, design some quick interventions that would have the desired effect.

Try these out the next time the opportunity arises.

51 Sizzling states at your fingertips!

Once you've mastered anchoring states, the possibilities for snapping into resourceful states whenever you wish are almost endless.

One of the best facilitators we know has set up a powerful cocktail of 'stacked' anchors using kinaesthetic triggers on their hand, so that they can simply access more of what they need to transform every learning event into something sizzling and magical.

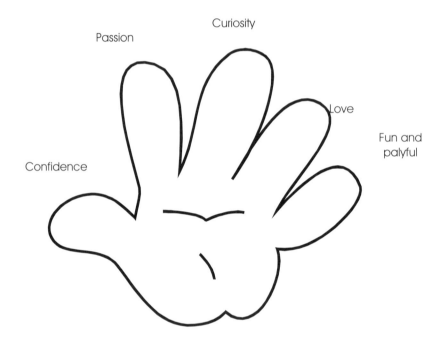

Passion

Curiosity

Love

Fun and palyful

Confidence

Activity: Your sizzling states

You can do the same. Choose five states that you know would make a really positive difference when you're facilitating and anchor them on your fingers. If you wish, use the list of states below for ideas. Don't choose states that already come easily to you in this situation – that's a waste! Choose states that are sometimes a struggle for you to access, and that would transform your resourcefulness and enjoyment.

The nice thing about anchors is that they become more powerful the more you use them, with each successful experience stacking on top of the one before. The good thing about installing anchors on your hand is that it is always with you!

Soon, you will automatically enter these states whenever you are about to begin training or facilitating – the situation itself becomes the anchor.

More resourceful states?

Amused	Delicious	Giggly	Marvellous	Sexy
Amorous	Delightful	Gobsmacked	Masculine	Surprised
Aroused	Deep	Glutted	Nice	Tasty
Abundant	Delectable	Happy	Needed	Tempted
Amazed	Dreamy	Horny	Natural	Together
Awesome	Elated	Healthy	Normal	Triumphant
Adventurous	Elegant	Heady	Nurtured	Tittilated
All right	Excellent	High	Nurturing	Tentimesbetter
Autonomous	Ecstatic	Hopeful	Open	Trusting
Bemused	Easy	Immense	Passionate	Understood
Brilliant	Energetic	Important	Playful	Unbelievable
Bountiful	Energized	Intense	Peaceofmind	Unstoppable
Blooming	Enigmatic	Infallible	Pleasure	Velvety
Beguiled	Empowered	Joyous	Powerful	Vibrant
Clever	Excited	Jubilant	Proud	VaVaVoom!
Celebratory	Free	Kindhearted	Primed	Vivacious
Careful	Fine	Kissable	Peaceful	Well
Cosy	Fantastic	Kooky	Prayerful	Wonderful
Comfortable	Frivolous	Knowledgeable	Protected	Wacky
Carefree	Funny	Kingly	Quiet	Wayout
Calm	Feminine	Loving	Quixotic	Weird
Charged	Funky	Lighthearted	Queenly	Wild
Cheerful	Grand	Limber	Quenched	Wicked
Chipper	Great	Loose	Randy	Xtragoodtoday
Confused	Gregarious	Luminous	Ready	Young
Congruent	Glad	Magnificent	Right	Youthful
Creative	Gigantic	Magnanimous	Restless	Zen
Crafty	Good	Magical	Rested	
Curious	Giddy	Masterful	Silly	

Less resourceful states?

Annoyed	Cantankerous	Defensive	Lazy
Angry	Crusty	Defeated	Malevolent
Animosity	Crabby	Disgruntled	Manic
Abandoned	Cranky	Desperate	Mad
Bad	Crappy	Disgusted	Miserable
Bored	Curmudgeonly	Embarrassed	Morbid
Baffled	Down	Guarded	Misunderstood
Blue	Dark	Glutted	Nasty
Barren	Dead (!)	Impotent	Obliged
Base	Degraded	Knackered	Obnoxious
Blah	Dejected	Lethargic	Overworked
Betrayed	Defenceless	Limited	Overtired

Overwhelmed   Possessive   Sapped   Timid
Offcolour   Ragged   Strange   Unsavoury
Offended   Rickety   Stupid   Underbatheweather
Old   Resentful   Stupefied   Wimpy
Pathetic   Raw   Stumped   Wasted
Pissedoff   Sad   Screwy   Woundup
Pitiful   Sick   Terrible   Xenophobic
Powerless   Sorrowful   Tricked

References

1. Howard Gardner (2000), *Intelligence Reframed: Multiple Intelligences for the 21st Century*, Basic Books.
2. James H. Gilmore and B. Joseph Pine II (1999), *The Experience Economy*, Harvard Business School Press.
3. David Kolb (1983), *Experiential Learning: Experience as the Source of Learning and Development*, Prentice Hall.
4. Peter Honey and Alan Mumford (1986), *Using Your Learning Styles*, Peter Honey Publications.
5. Bernice McCarthy (1987), *The 4MAT System: Teaching to Learning Styles*, Excel Inc.
6. Daniel Goleman (1996), *Emotional Intelligence*, Bloomsbury.
7. Carl Sagan (1974), *Broca's Brain*, Ballantine Books.
8. Nadine M. Weidman (1999), *Constructing Scientific Psychology: Karl Lashley's Mind-Brain Debates*, Cambridge Studies in the History of Psychology, Cambridge University Press.
9. Wilder Penfield (1975), *Mystery of the Mind: A Critical Study of Consciousness and the Human Brain*, Princeton University Press.
10. Eric Jensen (2000), *Brain-Based Learning*, The Brainstore Inc.
11. Benjamin Libet et al. (1999), *Volitional brain: Towards a Neuroscience of Free Will*, Imprint Academic.
12. Sharon Bartram and Brenda Gibson (1997), *Training Needs Analysis*, Gower.
13. Sam Goldstein (1998), *Overcoming Underachieving: An Action Guide to Helping Your Child Succeed in School*, John Wiley and Sons Ltd. Alternatively, see: www.samgoldstein.com
14. Donald L. Kirkpatrick (1998), *Evaluating Training Programs: The Four Levels*, Berrett-Koehler.
15. Sharon Bartram and Brenda Gibson (1999), *Evaluating Training*, Gower.
16. Tony Buzan (2000), *The Mind Map Book*, BBC Consumer Publishing.
17. B. Tuckman (1965), 'Developmental Sequence in Small Groups', *Psychological Bulletin*, **63**, pp. 384–99.
18. G. Pfurtscheller and A. Berghold (1989), 'Patterns of Cortical Activation During Planning of Voluntary Movement', *Electroencephalography and Clinical Neurophysiology*, **72**, pp. 250–58.
19. Eric Jensen (1995), *The Learning Brain*, The Brainstore Inc.
20. George A. Miller (1956), 'The Magical Number Seven Plus or Minus Two: Some Limits on our Capacity for Processing Information', *Psychological Review*, **101**(2), pp. 343–52.
21. Nelson Cowan (1977), *Attention and Memory: An Integrated Framework*, Oxford Psychology Series no. 26, Oxford University Press.
22. Gregory Bateson (1973), *Steps to an Ecology of Mind*, Paladin Books.
23. Gareth Morgan (1997), *Images of Organization*, Sage Publications.
24. Robert Rosenthal and Lenore Jacobson (1968), *Pygmalion in the Classroom*, Holt, Rinehart and Winston.
25. Renate N. Caine and Geoffrey Caine (1994), *Making Connections: Teaching and the Human Brain*, Addison-Wesley Publishing Co.
26. Mihalyi Csikszentmihalyi (1991), *Flow: The Psychology of Optimal Experience*, HarperCollins.
27. Georgi Lozanov (1978), *Suggestology and Outlines of Suggestology*, Gordon and Breach Science Publications.
28. Sheila Ostrander, Lynn Schroeder and Nancy Ostrander (1997), *Superlearning 2000*, Island Books.
29. Ole Anderson, Marcy Marsh and Dr Arthur Harvey (1999), *Learn with the Classics: Using Music to Study Smart at Any Age*, Lind Institute.
30. Steve Andreas and Connirae Andreas (1990), *Heart of the Mind*, Real People Press.

Further resources

Accelerated learning

Kaizen Training Limited (trainers' forum, trainers' tips, workshops, articles, resources)
www.kaizen-training.com

SEAL
The Society of Effective and Affective Learning (UK) (newsletter, annual conference, networking in the UK)
www.seal.org.uk

www.ialearn.org (conferences, articles, networking)
Headquarters for the International Alliance for Learning

Center for Accelerated Learning (publications, courses, course-design software)
Dave Meier
www.alcenter.com

Brainstore Inc. (Eric Jensen's outfit, based in California – great for brain research, supplies, articles and workshops)
www.thebrainstore.com

The Training Oasis
Another US site, but great for ideas on activities and energizers
www.sympatico.ca/thetrainingoasis

The Training Shop (great place in the UK to buy trainer resources)
www.thetrainingshop.co.uk

Bob Pike (creative training newsletter, supplies)
Creative Training Techniques
www.cttbobpike.com

Hermann International (brain dominance assessment, resources)
Ned Herrmann Group
www.hbdi.com

Russell Martin & Associates (workshops, articles)
www.russellmartin.com

Music and Learning

Dr Mark McKergow (great source for music to use when learning – and he's in the UK!)
www.mckergow.com

LifeSounds – Chris Brewer
music@flite.net

LIND Institute (good source for classical music)
Box 14487
San Francisco, CA 94114

Zephyr Press
www.zephyrpress.com

Mind Mapping®

www.buzancentres.com

Used with enthusiastic permission of The Buzan Organization Ltd.

www.mindmanager.co.uk (download a free trial of their Mind Mapping® software)

Aromas

Neema Vij
01932 240999
www.e2o.co.uk
neema@2o.co.uk